A Pair of Kings
and a Joker

A Pair of Kings and a Joker

James M. Hotchkiss, Jr.

Copyright © 2008 by James M. Hotchkiss, Jr.

ISBN: 978-0-557-00772-1

All rights reserved. No part of this book may be reproduced in any manner without written permission from the author, except in brief quotations used in articles or reviews.

This book was printed in the United States of America.

Table of Contents

CHAPTER 1
AN IMMIGRANT FAMILY 9

CHAPTER 2
CAMPBELLSVILLE 11

CHAPTER 3
ACROSS THE CONTINENT TO CALIFORNIA 14

CHAPTER 4
W. J. GETS STARTED 18

CHAPTER 5
EMMA 20

PHOTO SECTION 1
THE KING'S ANCESTORS AND DESCENDANTS 21

CHAPTER 6
TIME TO MOVE ON 40

CHAPTER 7
HE ALREADY DID ALL THIS 46

CHAPTER 8
CENTRAL CALIFORNIA CANNERIES 47

CHAPTER 9
DEL MONTE 56

CHAPTER 10
EVA BELL HITE, DOC WEAVER, NETTIE SNOOK AND CLEONE .. 60

PHOTO SECTION 2
THE KING'S BUSINESS 64

CHAPTER 11
MARIUS 77

CHAPTER 12
MARIUS AND THE LUMBER BUSINESS 87

CHAPTER 13
MARIUS AND HELENA 99

CHAPTER 14
TRY, TRY AGAIN 105

CHAPTER 15
THE CRUSIUS FAMILY 112

CHAPTER 16
KNIGHTSEN RANCH 116

CHAPTER 17
MEXICAN LAND CLAIM 121

CHAPTER 18
   BRIDGING THE GOLDEN GATE 123
CHAPTER 19
   POET, BUSINESSMAN, GOD 127
CHAPTER 20
   A LONG AND GLORIOUS PATHWAY TO OBSCURITY 134
CHAPTER 21
   THE KING IS DEAD 138
PHOTO SECTION 3
   THE JOKER AND THE YOUNG KING 142
CHAPTER 22
   LONG LIVE THE KING 158
CHAPTER 23
   HOTCHKISS ESTATE COMPANY 160
CHAPTER 24
   NICE GUYS FINISH LAST 166
CHAPTER 25
   DISTRIBUTION OF STOCK IN HOTCHKISS ESTATE COMPANY 170
CHAPTER 26
   THE RAPE OF EMMY LOU 175
CHAPTER 27
   FIREBAUGH FARMS 179
CHAPTER 28
   CHEEK AND HOTCHKISS 184
CHAPTER 29
   COVELO PONDEROSA PINE COMPANY 198
CHAPTER 30
   MILLER AND ME 201
CHAPTER 31
   EPIPHANY 205
CHAPTER 32
   ETHEL HOTCHKISS ESTATE 207
CHAPTER 33
   HOW COULD HE BE THE SON OF W.J.? 211
CHAPTER 34
   THE KINGS ARE GONE, BUT THE JOKER IS STILL WILD 218

CHAPTER 1

AN IMMIGRANT FAMILY

The sailing ship Hector arrived in 1638 with the two hundred people ready to found the New Haven Colony. It was another group of Puritans, ready to begin a new life in the new land. One of the passengers was fifteen year old Samuel Hotchkiss.

Samuel was on his own. His parents remained in Shropshire County, England. It would be nice to say that he became a model citizen and leader. In actuality, he was a boy, trying to find how to get along in the tough colonial world. The town records show that he was fined for having a dirty gun (twice), being absent from training, and twice sleeping on guard duty. With the danger of fire to the community ever present, Samuel was fined for not having a ladder to get to the top of his chimney.

The rules were strict, and they were strictly enforced. In September, 1642 the records show that Samuel Hotchkiss and Elizabeth Cleverly confessed their filthy dalliance together, and they were severely whipped. Two days later they applied for permission to be married even though they were under age.

The court really had no choice according to the records:
". . .and with all having entered into contact, sinfully and wickedly defiled each other with filthy dalliance and uncleane passages, by which they have both made themselves unfit for any other, and for which they have both received publique correction. . ." The court gave them permission to marry.

As the colony expanded, new lands were added, and Samuel got his small share. Never wealthy in any way, he died at the age of forty, leaving a small inheritance to his widow and six minor children. The transition from immigrant family to citizen family was completed. Samuel's five sons and a daughter married well, raised families and served their community. The adventuring and pioneering begun by Samuel stopped temporarily, but it would continue in a family line that eventually found W. J. Hotchkiss crossing the plains from Kentucky to California in a covered wagon two centuries later.

Samuel's oldest son John was twenty years old when his father died. The burden of caring for Elizabeth and the younger children fell on him. Because of the responsibilities, he did not marry until he was twenty-nine years old. He died seventeen years later, the youngest of his seven children being one year old at his death.

Large families were characteristic in Colonial times. The older children helped the younger, and everybody pitched in to do something to help the family survive the arduous life. However, a community can grow to be pretty large after two generations. New lands were needed. There were no trains or buses, and there were hostile Indians. The new town had to be established by a planned, simultaneous move of several families. The maximum distance of the move was fifteen miles. This permitted the establishment of a road connecting back to the original settlement.

Samuel's grandson, Josiah, was born in 1680. He continued the pioneer spirit by moving from New Haven to Cheshire, a distance of fourteen miles. When the road between the towns became secure, he established a tavern outside of Cheshire. There were many dangers that threatened pioneers and non-pioneers alike. Josiah and his wife died in a smallpox epidemic.

The pioneering spirit took another rest after Josiah's death. His son, grandson, and great grandson in the direct line were all buried in Cheshire.

Benoni Hotchkiss was Josiah's great great grandson. Born in Cheshire in 1794, he was one of the many young men who moved out of New England in the early nineteenth century to seek their fortune elsewhere. In history, these young men are known as "Yankee Traders". Somehow, Benoni found his way to Campbellsville, Kentucky and established himself as the first merchant in central Kentucky. With a sign of the brilliance that was to spring forth later in his grandson, he assured his future by marrying the daughter of the town's founder.

CHAPTER 2

CAMPBELLSVILLE

Adam Campbell and his brothers, David and James, founded the town of Campbellsville, Kentucky in 1817 according to Collins History of Kentucky. Only Adam stayed. He and his wife, Sally (Steele) Campbell built a plantation about one mile out of town. Both came from Virginia. Their ancestry was Scotch, Adam from the highlands and Sally from the lowlands.

The plantation consisted of a large log house, several immense barns and stables plus a mill and a distillery. A local resident wrote that Adam Campbell was a benevolent, intelligent man. When he was justice of the peace, he always tried to get the litigants to settle their cases out of court.

Sally had an interesting background. Her gr gr grandfather was Sir Richard Steele, who was born in Dublin, Ireland in 1672. The family was Scotch-Irish. Three of Richard's sons immigrated to Virginia and established themselves in the Shenandoah Valley in Augusta County. Two generations later Sally's father, James Steele, was a lieutenant in the Revolutionary War. James' brother David, also a war veteran, established Steele's Tavern. The tavern was a post office and a stage stop halfway between Staunton and Lexington. Staunton was the county seat of Augusta County.

Adam Campbell and Sally were married in Staunton before starting their move to Kentucky. They are the grandparents of W.J. Hotchkiss. The connection to the Shenandoah was reestablished when W.J. married Emma Grove, who was also from Staunton.

Adam and Sally were not fortunate in their family. They had nine children, of whom two died in infancy. Only Jane, the eldest, lived a long and prolific life. With her husband, Benoni Hotchkiss, she produced seven children and lived to the age of eighty-two.

Something bad happened to all six of Sally's other children. Mary delivered three children but died at the age of twenty-three. The other children also died relatively young. Before he died, Adam saw the death of four of his nine children. Sally lived on to see four more die.

Jane Campbell and Benoni Hotchkiss were married in Campbellsville December 4, 1823. Benoni had wandered far from his birthplace to find a successful business, a new home, and a strong young wife from a pioneer family, who came complete with an inheritance. His children had all the comforts and a chance to marry well.

On August 8, 1913 the Taylor County Enquirer printed a memoir by Jack Harding, an old time resident. The article included capsule descriptions of three daughters of Jane and Benoni:

"Lois [Hotchkiss] married Hon. A. J. Gowdy, and the Gowdys of Campbellsville are descended from them. A. J. Gowdy, a man of fine ability, was a surveyor, merchant, tobacconist and member of the legislature. His wife, Lois, was a bright and beautiful lady. She always kept a fine saddle horse, and I never saw a finer horsewoman.

"Mag, a beautiful lady, tall graceful, married Jack Sanders. The line is extinct. Eliza was a charming lady with golden chestnut hair, and always bright, cheerful and happy. Dr. J. B. Buchanan is her son. Her second husband was Dr. Sam Chandler, a delicate man most of his life, he was one of the finest physicians in Kentucky. There is talent in this family."

Talent indeed! The three sisters are uniformly described as bright as well as beautiful. Eliza's son became a doctor, and Eliza married a doctor the second time around. Lois, in addition to being a great horsewoman, married the leading merchant in town.

In another part of the article the author mentions the fourth sister, Emma, who married Dr. Irvine, a big man with a big heart and brain.

Benoni Hotchkiss, Sr. died in Campbellsville August 1, 1849. At that time, Benoni, Jr. was not quite sixteen years old. As he described himself in 1880 in his submission to *History of Sonoma County, California, Illustrated:*

"Young Benoni then left to his own inclination and an indulgent mother, followed the divers pursuits which most settlers fancy, until he became of age and acquired his patrimony. On January 8, 1857 he was married to Virginia, daughter of Jane and Barrett Edrington. With a number of others he crossed the plains in 1860 and first settled in Yolo County, near Knights Landing on the Sacramento River."

CHAPTER 3

ACROSS THE CONTINENT TO CALIFORNIA

The decision to move two thousand miles away was not an easy one. William Josephus (W. J.) Hotchkiss was born October 20, 1858. A year later Virginia prepared to deliver twins. During the birth process one twin died and lay across the other one. Janie was born paralyzed from the waist down. In her later photographs she looked many years younger than her brother. Virginia survived, but she never had any more children.

Virginia was the third of eleven children of Barrett Edrington and Jane (Kerr) Edrington. Jane's eleventh child was born when the mother was forty-four years old. The next pregnancy in 1858 was twins. Jane and both twins died.

The group that moved west was more than Benoni and Virginia plus their two children. It also included Barrett Edrington and his nine other children plus Barrett's brother. The entire Edrington family was headed west. At the age of twenty-two, Virginia had maternal responsibility for her two year old son, her crippled one year old daughter, her father and her nine siblings, which included a five year old and a three year old. Interestingly, the five and three year olds were the uncle and aunt of Virginia's children. The only female adult help for Virginia was her oldest sister, who had her own one year old twins to care for.

Fortunately, the cross country trip was well organized and uneventful. The family traveled first from Kentucky to Missouri, where they stayed for several months, getting organized. The leader of the party actually combined two relatively large groups into one very large group. He was an experienced leader, and there were no surprises along the way. The most exciting event was when they passed Pike's Peak, and several members of the party climbed it.

In later years Virginia spoke often of the parties around the campfire, folk dancing and all. However, she would never go on a picnic. She said she had had all the picnicking she ever wanted already. All her meals along the wagon train route included caring for six pre school children. That could take all of the fun out of a picnic.

The family could well have stayed in Kentucky. Benoni had sufficient resources to start a business or buy a farm, but the war clouds were already overhead. He was confident there was going to be a civil war. Although the family was loyal to the Southern cause, they opposed secession. They also feared that Kentucky might side with the North, and Benoni might have to fight the South. When they heard of Lincoln's election in 1860, they had already left Kentucky.

The pioneer spirit had risen in Benoni. His two thousand mile journey across country was in the same spirit and probably took about the same amount of courage as Josiah Hotchkiss' fifteen mile move to Cheshire and Benoni Senior's one thousand mile move to Campbellsville. The excitement of adventure was embedded in the family blood, in the heart, and certainly it pervaded the atmosphere in their homes. It was the motivator for W.J. with his many adventures in the business world. One generation later Hazel Hotchkiss, the internationally famous tennis champion, attributed her strong competitive spirit to her pioneer families.

When the group reached California, they thought they owned a farm in Yolo County near Knights Landing on the Sacramento River. However, title to the land was clouded, and it was eventually lost.

The next stop was the nearby city of Woodland. There Benoni built the first hotel in town. The family was always clear about their sympathy to the South in the Civil War. The hotel was the site of many Southern balls planned by Virginia. When Lincoln died, Virginia refused to drape the hotel in black. Shortly thereafter, perhaps by popular demand, the hotel was sold, and the family moved to its final destination.

Moving to California had been a difficult decision for Barrett Edrington. He had capital, like Benoni. He could have stayed in Kentucky. He was fifty-one years old. The pioneer spirit does not burn as brightly at that age, but it was in his blood. His great grandfather had emigrated from England. Maybe it was time to put the death of his wife behind him and take the whole family to a brand new area.

It was obvious that Barrett was the leader of the group rather than Benoni, although Benoni certainly was willing to go along. If you are twenty-seven years old and you hear your father-in-law say he is taking all of his ten children to California, you better go with him.

The families stayed together for quite a while. Barrett had a farm in Yolo County while Benoni had the hotel. One of Barrett's chores during the period of hotel ownership was to look for possible farms for Benoni to purchase. He recommended a site on the Russian River in the Sotoyome District, south of Healdsburg. The property consisted of 375 acres, including 125 acres of river bottom land. Apples and walnuts were raised in the higher elevation. The bottom land was planted to prunes. For many years a sign on the railroad station in Healdsburg stated proudly, "Healdsburg, The Buckle of the Prune Belt."

It was a while before the various Edringtons moved away. Several of them are recorded as attending the Sotoyome School, which served Benoni's property. Barrett eventually moved to Shasta County, near the headwaters of the Sacramento River, where he died in 1871. His children established families of their own in various parts of Northern California.

It took Benoni several months to get from Kentucky to California. After the transcontinental railroad came, it took him only a few days to return to Kentucky. He went back to visit several times, each time for the purpose of talking his brother David Josephus (Joe) into coming to California. David had been widowed in 1863, but he resolutely refused to move. He died in Campbellsville.

Barrett Edrington also went back to Kentucky to visit. He had no more recruiting success than Benoni, but he had already moved his entire family to California. When he lived in Kentucky, Barrett had been an overseer on a tobacco plantation. The black workers were not slaves. Both in 1860 and after the war the workers asked Barrett to take them all with him to California, but it was an impossible task.

Benoni and Virginia had reached the end of the trail. They spent the remainder of their lives on their farm, living quietly and as good neighbors.

Virginia's baby brother, James Barrett Edrington, (Jim B.) stayed on until he married about 1900. He and his wife returned to stay and raise his family soon afterwards, living on the ranch until his death in 1946. W.J. Hotchkiss grew up and took over much of the management of the ranch in the 1880's. Benoni, with Edrington help, had earlier built a home for the family. It was replaced by a newer and larger home in the 1880's. W.J. did the planning. Jim B. hauled much of the lumber by wagon from Guerneville, twenty miles downstream on the Russian River. The house was mentioned in one of the histories of Sonoma County as one of the finest in the area.

Life in the nineteenth century was hard. Benoni avoided a lot of the most arduous work, but pioneering is never easy. A photograph of the family was taken in 1890 in front of the new house. Benoni wore a long gray beard and looked as if he was well over seventy years old. He was fifty-seven at the time. Janie had died three years before, at the age of twenty-eight. Benoni lived eight more years. He died May 23, 1898 at the age of sixty-five.

Benoni and Janie are buried in the Hotchkiss plot at Oak Mound Cemetery in Healdsburg, California. It is a beautiful grave site under hundred year old redwood trees, probably planted at the time of Janie's death. Virginia lived on for many years. She died December 12, 1927 at the age of eighty-nine.

CHAPTER 4

W. J. GETS STARTED

Benoni's son was usually called Joe. He was never called William or Josephus. In the business world he was known as W.J. most of the time, but there were many times when he stuck with Joe. Although he was raised on a farm, Joe was not isolated. His mother was quite active with the local social and charitable organizations. The town of Healdsburg was only a couple of miles away. The elementary school was closer. If he needed to look for companionship at any time, there was Barrett Edrington's giant brood. Of course there were farm chores but not back breaking labor for a child. In the farm world, this family had to be considered well-to-do.

He went to high school in Healdsburg, then to business school in Santa Rosa, fifteen miles away. After a year of that, Joe made his first important decision, no more business school. "They're trying to make me into a bookkeeper," he lamented.

The next step was to go to the county courthouse, take a qualifying examination and receive a certificate that permitted him to be a teacher. He taught at the Starr School in nearby Windsor for a year. After his one year stint, he found there was plenty to do running the family farm. Benoni was only 47 years old in 1880, but the years had fallen hard on him. He needed his son's help.

In the 1880's Joe designed and supervised the building of the new and larger ranch home. In that same decade he also married and fathered five children. However, there was still time available to begin building his empire. The characteristics that made him successful were already in place. He simply liked people. They were all equal in his eyes, and he enjoyed them all. Humor both dry and rich filled his conversation and his correspondence. He was a happy man. He had fun, and his tolerance was broad. He had a real desire to help others. His knowledge was freely given. He liked to see others working and striving, and he was delighted to help them reach their goals. The people whose lives he touched liked him. They felt his warmth and sincerity. Everybody associated with him at every level must have felt the enthusiasm of W.J. Hotchkiss. Even people who lost money in one of Joe's many business ventures continued to like him.

A common characteristic of many great men is the intense desire to acquire knowledge. Joe was an avid reader. The lack of a college education was not an impediment. In each of his business activities he quickly learned the necessary technical knowledge. He already carried the knowledge of life.

The start was simple and very close to home. Jim Miller, also a second generation farmer, lived on the adjacent farm. He and W.J. went into the prune drying business. They were their own best customers, since both farms grew prunes. They also offered custom drying service to other farmers in the area.

Joe and Jim were such good friends that they agreed to name their first born sons after each other. James Miller Hotchkiss was Joe's first born. Joe Hotchkiss Miller was his counterpart. The friendship of the two farmers was more successful than their prune drying business. Eventually, Jim Miller gave up farming and moved to Seattle where he worked in the ceramic tile business.

W.J. had no trouble moving onward and upward after the prunes. Once a business was established, he often lost interest. He was ready for the next opportunity. In today's world he would be called a promoter-developer and possibly also an adventurer. Remembering that he was not a bookkeeper, he left little personal trail of where he had been. Sometimes he moved in and out so fast that his activities appeared only as rumors.

We know very little about his "cornering" the salt market in California in the 1890's. We know only that he participated in the Alaskan gold rush at the turn of the century. The only evidence was his gift of a gold nugget to his daughter. It is easier to adventure close to home, so he and Jim Miller established a winery near the Starr School in the 1880's.

CHAPTER 5

EMMA

Emma's uncle, Gus Hite, was an original 49er in California. Gus built the first hotel in Yosemite Valley. He then built an ambitious two story inn and stayed to manage it. This is the inn that was acquired by James Mason Hutchings, the prominent author and promoter of the beauties of Yosemite Valley. Gus sold out because he had to help his brother. John Hite made a major gold discovery downstream on the Merced River in 1861. He asked Gus to help build the mining town and a hotel. John also sent to Virginia for three nephews to help with the mine. A few years later, with that much of the family already in California, John wanted to complete the move. He arranged for the purchase of a prune ranch near Healdsburg. It just happened to be the ranch next door to the Miller ranch, one ranch away from the Hotchkiss ranch. John's sister Lucretia and her husband, James Rankin Grove, moved there along with their daughter Emma and Emma's two younger brothers. The trip by transcontinental railroad in 1875 was easy.

The railroad was great for moving from one city to another. It was not flexible for moving around after you got there. Automobiles had not been invented, so the horse and buggy came into play. In that rural environment young men were inclined to take a good look at the girl next door. It was easier to court the girl who lived close by. It was better than traveling a couple of hours each way for a date.

W.J. courted Emma. She was the girl almost next door, from the other ranch down the road. W.J would go out in his rig with his horse, because he had no automobile. He would park in front of the house. Emma was always late like any other woman. W.J. was happy to point out the spot where the horse had impatiently kept pawing at the tree. Then he walked around to the other side of the tree and showed the spot where he had started pawing impatiently at the tree, kicking it with his foot. The tree survived, as did the relationship. The two were married November 25, 1880. He was 22 years old; she was 27.

Grandparents of W.J. Hotchkiss

Sarah Jane (Campbell) Hotchkiss
b 12/24/1806 d 3/19/1889

Benoni Hotchkiss, Sr.
b 5/8/1794   d 8/1/1849

About 1863 Virginia, Janie, and W.J.

W.J.'s Mother, Virginia

James Rankin Grove
Emma's Father

Lucretia (Hite) Grove
Emma's Mother

Hotchkiss plot, Oak Mound Cemetery, Healdsburg, CA.
The redwood trees were planted at the time of Benoni's daughter's death in 1887

Marius Hotchkiss and siblings about 1890
Left to Right; Linville, J. Miller, Homer, Marius, Hazel

3 Generations of the Hotchkiss Family at their ranch home near Healdsburg, CA, about 1890. Left to right: Front Row; Hazel, Linville: Middle row; James Miller, Marius, Homer Back row: W. J. (William Josephus), Emma; To the side: Virginia, Benoni, unknown.

Hazel and brothers about 1905.
Back row: Miller, Homer, Marius
Front row: Linville, Hazel.

They called themselves the ten grandchildren of W. J. Hotchkiss.
Miller, George, Emmy Lou, Hazel, Virginia, Bill, Pete, Dotty, Bill, Jim.

About 1926 at W. J. Hotchkiss House,
2985 Claremont Avenue, Berkeley, California.

Standing left to right:

Miller F. Hotchkiss (Marius' son)
Linville Hotchkiss (Marius' brother)
Helena (Crusius) Hotchkiss (Marius' wife)
Margaret (Locan) Hotchkiss (Linville's wife)
Margaretta (Wilson) Hotchkiss (J. Miller's wife)
Hazel (Hotchkiss) Wightman
J. Miller Hotchkiss (Marius' brother)
George Wightman, Hazel's son
George William Wightman, Hazel's husband
Marius Hotchkiss

Middle Row:

Bill Hotchkiss (J. Miller's son)
Emma (Grove) Hotchkiss (Marius' mother) holding Bill Wightman (Hazel's son)
W. J. (Joe) Hotchkiss (Marius' father)
John Peter Hotchkiss (Linville's son)

Front Row:

Hazel Wightman (Hazel's daughter)
Dorothy Wightman (Hazel's daughter)
Virginia Wightman (Hazel's daughter)

James Rankin Grove
b: 2/13/1822   d: 8/8/1886
m: Lucretia Virginia Hite
b: 2/20/1823   d: 5/9/1914

Emma Lucretia Grove
b: 8/22/1853   d: 7/27/1936

William Josephus Hotchkiss
b: 10/20/1858   d: 11/2/1936

Marius William Hotchkiss b: 11/5/1884   d: 3/1/1974

Miller Francis Hotchkiss b: 11/27/1910   d: 2/27/1968

Barrett Edrington
b: 2/1/1809   d: 10/17/1881
m: Jane Kerr
b: 11/22/1813   d: 12/22/1858

Virginia Edrington
b: 11/12/1838   d: 12/12/1927
m: Benoni Hotchkiss
b: 12/20/1833   d: 5/23/1898

Descendants of William Josephus Hotchkiss

29 Nov 2007

1. William Josephus Hotchkiss (b.20 Oct 1858-Campbellsville,,Kentucky;d.2 Nov 1936-Berkeley,Alameda Co.,CA)
    sp: Emma Lucretia Grove (b.20 Aug 1853-Staunton,Augusta Co.,Virginia;m.25 Nov 1880;d.27 Jul 1936-Berkeley,Alameda Co.,CA)
    2. James Miller Hotchkiss (b.23 Sep 1881-Healdsburg,,CA;d.17 Nov 1952-Berkeley,,CA)
        sp: Margaretta Wilson (b.4 Oct 1885-Del Norte,Rio Grande Co.,Colorado;m.23 Jun 1917;d.18 Apr 1962-Oakland,,California)
        3. William Joseph (Bill) Hotchkiss (b.8 Apr 1919-Berkeley,,California;d.10 Dec 1972-Berkeley,,California)
            sp: Margaret (Peggy) Douglas (b.16 Feb 1919-Point Fermin,L,Calif.;m.19 Aug 1939;d.30 Jun 2007-Oakley,CCC,CA)
        3. James Miller Hotchkiss Jr. (b.16 Jan 1927-Oakland,Alameda Co.,California)
            sp: Isabel Gandarillas Moruza (b.22 Apr 1925-Westwood,Lassen Co.,California;m.19 Jun 1948)
    2. Homer Grove Hotchkiss (b.4 Mar 1883-Healdsburg,Sonoma Co.,CA;d.2 Aug 1924-Berkeley,Alameda Co.,CA)
        sp: Edna Shirley McVay (b.1893-,,Oregon;m.16 Oct 1913)
        3. Emmy Lou Hotchkiss (b.26 Aug 1914-Pleasanton,,California;d.8 Jan 1980-Sacramento,,California)
            sp: Samuel Griffith Hanson (b.27 Apr 1912-,,Oregon;m.28 Dec 1938;d.18 Jan 1989-Sacramento,,California)
    2. Marius William Hotchkiss (b.5 Nov 1884-Healdsburg,,CA;d.1 Mar 1974-Berkeley,,CA)
        sp: Helena Barbara Crusius (b.7 Dec 1889-Crescent City,,California;m.19 Dec 1909;d.23 Mar 1968-Berkeley,,California)
        3. Miller Francis Hotchkiss (b.27 Nov 1910;d.27 Feb 1968-Firebaugh,Madera Co.,California)
            sp: Marjorie Burns (b.2 Mar 1912-,,Montana;m.(Div);d.6 Jun 1967-Kentfield,Marin Co.,CA)
    2. Hazel Virginia Hotchkiss (b.20 Dec 1886-Healdsburg,Sonoma Co.,CA;d.5 Dec 1974-Chestnut Hill,,Mass.)
        sp: George William Wightman (b.17 Dec 1890-Jamaica Plain,,Mass.;m.24 Feb 1912(Div);d.25 May 1963)
        3. George Wightman (b.4 Dec 1912-Brookline,,MA;d.16 Feb 1978)
            sp: Virginia Mayo Dyer (b.4 Oct 1912-Hingham,,MA;m.5 Nov 1937(Div);d.24 Apr 1966)
        3. Virginia Wightman (b.1 Jul 1914-Brookline,MA;d.16 Jul 2000-Niantic,CT)
            sp: Robert Turner Henckel (b.14 Apr 1908-New York,,New York;m.3 Dec 1938;d.3 Jun 1984-Yonkers,NY)
        3. Hazel Hotchkiss Wightman (b.11 Jun 1916;d.16 Jan 2004-Evanston,IL)
            sp: Albert Mason Jr. Harlow (b.20 Apr 1916-Concord,,Mass.;m.28 Mar 1942(Div);d.18 Jun 1977)
        3. Dorothy Wightman (b.23 Feb 1922;d.31 Aug 2005-San Francisco,CA)
            sp: William Benson Peavey (b.27 Oct 1920;m.19 Mar 1944(Div);d.18 Dec 1999-Colma,CA)
            sp: Leslie Hood (m.17 Dec 1965(Div))
        3. William Hotchkiss Wightman (b.2 Sep 1925;d.30 Sep 1991-Boston,,Mass.)
            sp: Sally Delano (b.1 Oct 1923;m.28 Apr 1951)
    2. Linville Lee Hotchkiss (b.9 Nov 1888-Healdsburg,,CA;d.21 Nov 1962-Riverside Co. CA (resided Coachella))
        sp: Margaret Locan (b.17 Jun 1891;m.5 Aug 1916(Div);d.17 Feb 1952-Carmel,,California)
        3. John Peter (Pete) Hotchkiss (b.22 Apr 1920;d.23 Dec 1944-,,,Belgium)
        sp: Dorothy Erwin (m.Abt 1906(Div))
        sp: Dorothy L. Houston (m.1908(Div))
        sp: Ethel Trout (m.Aft 1940)

W. J. at Bohemian Grove

W. J. Hotchkiss about 1915

W. J. Hotchkiss at various ages

Emma (Grove) Hotchkiss at 1924 Democratic national convention.

Emma Hotchkiss

On Mount Tamalpais – March 12, 1911
The plank walk wood was supposed to be easier for ladies in their "fragile shoes".
Hazel (Hotchkiss) Wightman second from left
Emma (Grove) Hotchkiss far right
Hazel, famous in her own right, had already won several of her many national tennis championships. Her biography, First Lady of Tennis, by Tom Carter was published in 2001.

JAMES M. HOTCHKISS, JR. 39

This group photo was taken about March, 1914 on the tennis court that W. J. built for his daughter, Hazel, the national tennis champion.

The picture was carefully preserved by Emmy Lou (Hotchkiss) Hanson. It includes her father Homer, and a rare photo of her mother Edna (Mc Vay) Hotchkiss.

Hazel is at front center. After all, it is her court. Homer, holding racket, is third from left. Edna is fourth form right. Emma, obviously not dressed for tennis, is far right. Emmy Lou is not visible. The photo was taken six months before she was born

CHAPTER 6

TIME TO MOVE ON

W.J. continued the expansion of his various businesses. He rented office space in San Francisco and hired a secretary. His problem was that there was no satisfactory way to communicate with his office and his business associates. His phone connection was a basic country party line. Mail service took two to three days. To make a personal visit, he had to get to the ferry terminal by wagon and then take a long boat trip to the Ferry Building in San Francisco. It was no accident that his office was within walking distance of the waterfront.

Not surprisingly, W.J. greeted the turn of the century with plans to move his residence to the San Francisco Bay Area. Since he had two sons in college in Berkeley, he settled there. He still had to take a ferry ride across the bay, but there were connecting commuter trains along several Berkeley and Oakland routes.

The family lived for a year in rented property close to the University of California campus, while they went house looking. They found their dream house, moved in, and lived there the rest of their lives. The five children and ten grandchildren always referred to it as "The Big House". It was indeed large. On the ground floor there were three separate parlors, a dining room, large pass-pantry, and a massive kitchen. In the second story, there were six large bedrooms and three bathrooms. The third floor had storage areas and a very large finished room, which included permanently installed exercise rings and parallel bars.

For no particular reason, there was a separate room that might have been used as a separate bedroom.

The house climaxed on the fourth floor in a cupola with windows looking in all four directions with a grand view. The cupola was likewise visible to many of the surrounding residents. In the year 1932 Emma trudged up the stairs and hung on a box frame four life size posters of presidential candidate Franklin Delano Roosevelt.

In front of the house was a heart shaped lawn with a driveway all around, connecting to the beginning of the main driveway that led from the boulevard to the large garage and the side and rear entrances of the house. Between the two driveways was a good sized island landscaped with tall shrubs. The main driveway wound down a short but relatively steep hill to one of the many creeks that flowed through Berkeley. A wooden bridge made it possible to cross the creek and climb the gentler hill on the other side until it reached a city street.

The garage was originally a stable. The full time gardener lived in a room on the second floor. The hill dropped ten feet sharply at the back of the garage. The lower level was also used for storage. At the back of the house was a partially finished storage shed. Nearby was a lath house where Emma personally used gasoline to dry clean the family's clothes. W.J. planted several eucalyptus trees, which grew quite tall in the favorable Berkeley climate. He had also planted a single eucalyptus at the roadside in Healdsburg. A hundred years later that tree is used as a landmark for the entrance to the property.

The change in housing from Healdsburg to Berkeley was not considerable. The big rambling two story ranch house was also roomy and comfortable. It only had two parlors, but it also had several bedrooms and a large kitchen. With typical foresight, W.J. had placed it on a small knoll that protected it from the occasional flooding of the Russian River. The big difference was that the commuter train had a regularly scheduled stop right in front of the Berkeley house. The comfortable trains ran to the waterfront destination, where all of the routes met at the ferry pier. W.J. could go to work in the morning and come home in the evening, just like a real city dweller.

The housing change was easy. What was difficult to do was provide care for his mother and care for his ranch.

Jim B. was the youngest of the Edrington brood. As Barrett and the rest slowly drifted away, Jim B. stayed on. He did a major portion of the hauling of logs from Guerneville for the building of the ranch house in the 1880's. As Virginia's baby brother, he had special status in the household, but he never seemed to have any special managerial responsibility. It was a comfortable existence for him, and the years passed by. Suddenly, unexpectedly his world changed.

Benoni was consistent when he took his return trips to Kentucky. He always tried to recruit new citizens for California. Eventually in 1898 Thomas Cook arrived along with his son Ben and his nineteen year old daughter, Hattie. Ben's wife Meg was also in the group. W.J. had planned for Ben to work on the ranch, but Meg said she hated California. Hattie stayed on the ranch with Virginia, but Ben and Meg went back to Kentucky.

The forty-three year old Jim B. was smitten with Hattie. For a short period his life was changed. The two married and moved to Los Gatos, where Jim B. found work as a gardener. They did not stay long in Los Gatos. Once again, W.J. Hotchkiss was able to come up with a plan that was a win-win for everybody. Benoni had died in 1898. Virginia had shown no interest in leaving her home, and W.J. needed to provide for her comfort. He contacted Jim B. and told him that if he and Hattie would come back to the ranch and make a home for Virginia, W.J. would see that all their children were educated.

Virginia was fond of both Jim B. and Hattie, so the arrangement would be best for her. Jim B. had proved to be unemployable at other than minimal jobs, so it would be a step up for him. With the first child on the way, there was added reason to come back home. In a world where scholarships were minimal, this was a magnificent opportunity for the children. Jim B. lived on the ranch until he died at the age of ninety-one. Every year he cultivated his vegetable garden. He was never quite sure of the new fangled stuff. Long after indoor plumbing came to the house, he continued to take his Montgomery Ward catalog to the outhouse every morning.

Hattie was cared for by her children after Jim B. died. She lived to the age of eighty-eight.

It was a true fairytale for Lorena, the oldest child. She attended the University of California at Berkeley. While there she lived with W.J. and Emma part of the time, spending time also at her sorority. She majored in bacteriology and had a distinguished career working for the City of San Francisco. She married but had no children.

In the year 1936 Lorena received a special assignment. Her department had been asked to do some special tests on a hospital patient in Berkeley. She walked into the room to say hello, and there was W. J. It would have been an unbelievably heart warming story if Lorena's work had saved W.J.'s life, but it didn't. He died a few months later. On the other hand, Lorena lived on past the age of one hundred after a great career.

Horace Edrington chose to go to the University of California at Davis. There he learned two important things, how to care for cows and how to play the trumpet. When he graduated, he knew which was more important. He went on the road for three years with the Dick Jergens dance band. It was a wonderful idyll, which ended when Horace finally decided the road life was not for him. Although he was a good musician and could have always found musical employment, he decided to settle down and use the other stuff he learned at Davis.

Why not do something on the ranch? W. J. Hotchkiss respected entrepreneurial vision much more than musical ability. He was pleased to loan money to Horace for setting up a dairy. The loan was subsequently repaid. It paid for a small milking barn with six stalls, fourteen jersey cows, modern milk processing building, and a daily delivery truck. Edrington's Jersey Dairy was in business.

Horace had one man as a helper. The two of them milked the cows every morning. The milk was brought into the building where it was poured into a large stainless steel container. From there it flowed down over a flash cooler and fell ice cold into a ten gallon can. The cans were then stored in the large walk-in refrigerator. Milk was delivered in glass bottles at that time. Returned bottles were thoroughly washed and dried and then placed in a case that held twelve bottles of one quart size. Preparing for the delivery route, Horace poured milk from a ten gallon can into the hand bottler. The bottler had a pressure nipple on the bottom to prevent overflow. Each of the twelve bottles was filled in turn. The capper was a simple little machine that was placed on top of the bottle. A push on the lever delivered one cap for each bottle.

The filled cases were loaded into the truck and covered with damp burlap. It was time for the delivery route to begin. The route boy at one time was Lyden Mothorn, a cousin. He carried the delivery to the appropriate location at each house and brought back the empty bottles. The route was finished around noon. It was time for lunch and Horace's well earned afternoon nap. Then at five in the afternoon the whole process started all over again, ending with the evening route. He got to bed after ten to be rested for the start of the next day at five a.m.

There were no days off and no time for illness. It was very hard work but also very rewarding. Horace was there every day, personally involved at every step of the process. Dating a lady was something that was barely possible. He would leave right after the evening delivery and not return until time for the morning milking. After a while, Horace and Eunice got married. He got more sleep at night, and he had also found a bookkeeper.

Eventually, the hard work paid off. No more twice a day delivery routes for this couple, they went into the wholesale milk business in Marin County near Olema. The ten gallon cans stayed in the refrigerator until the big truck from the big dairy picked them up. For retirement Horace and Eunice returned to Healdsburg and a comfortable home on West Dry Creek Road. They both lived into their nineties.

Horace was fun, and he was kind, an unbeatable combination. When visitors came to see the original dairy operation, he had a special treat for them. He would hand them a gill bottle. Gill is a unit of measure that has pretty much fallen out of use these days. It still is an eighth of a quart or four fluid ounces. In those days Horace had a few bottles that were gill size, tiny little things. He would let the visitor hold the little bottle under the flash cooler and catch the milk before it went into the ten gallon can. The milk was really fresh. It had been inside the cow a few minutes earlier. When it went into the bottle, it was cool; it was fresh; it was wonderful. That is the way to remember Horace Edrington. Fresh and unspoiled, he was wonderful. He was a real cool guy.

After getting Jim B. in place, W.J. still had a problem with the management of the ranch. He kept it in the family by reaching back to Campbellsville for his first cousin, Dave Hotchkiss. A generation earlier Dave's father, David Josephus, had refused to join Benoni in California. This generation was different. W.J. offered Dave a job as general manager of the ranch, and Dave accepted. He was surely influenced by his wife, Bettie, who was Hattie's half sister. Bettie's father, Ben Cook, had gone to California along with Hattie. It would be good to be reunited. It was another success for W.J. He had found his ranch manager and his mother's manager, and they were tied together and bound to the ranch by the Cook family connection.

Dave assumed the manager's role and performed well. He bought a small piece of adjacent land on the other side of the hill from the ranch. Bettie and Dave built their house and raised their five children there. Dave walked over the hill to get to work. He managed the ranch until his retirement. Bettie often walked over the hill to visit Hattie.

Dave's Sister, Eliza, had married Robert Jones in Kentucky. They figured they might just as well move to California also. One of their children was Tom Jones, who went to work for W.J. He was a very valuable employee, applying his excellent analytical abilities in the evaluation of old and new investments.

CHAPTER 7

HE ALREADY DID ALL THIS

W.J. found many outlets for his boundless energy before he left Healdsburg. In 1887 he served a two year term in the California State Assembly without particular distinction. That was the only time he sought political office. He probably considered that political service got in his way. He wanted to do all kinds of other things that he didn't have time for. He did make a few hundred new friends, which certainly did not hurt his future business career.

When we last heard of the wine business, W.J. owned a winery in Windsor near the Starr School. In the search for economies of scale, the one winery soon became three. W.J. helped organize the California Wine Makers Corporation in 1894 and became its general manager. This was essentially an organization owned by wine growers and dedicated to lobbying and promotion. It was the first of many opportunities to exploit the connections with the legislature. Wine making profits had been deplorable. It took W.J. only six years to turn the industry around. Amidst industry wide acclaim, he could have established a permanent bureaucracy with him in charge for a lifetime. That was not his entrepreneurial way. Instead, he helped terminate the corporation in the year 1900. This was one of the very few times in history that a bureaucracy declined and died.

All of W.J.'s businesses had humble beginnings, but they did not stay humble for very long. Central California Canneries began with a very small cannery in Healdsburg. By the time of the move, there were three large canneries in Sacramento, Emeryville and Sebastopol. Already, it was the second largest canning company in California. In 1902 at the California State Fair gold medals were won by Central California Canneries for the best canned goods and the best equipped canneries in the state. Future chapters will be devoted to the continued growth of Central California Canneries after W.J. moved to the Bay Area.

The lumber business was acquired in 1902. This large story is also deferred to later chapters along with major acquisitions of farmland in the San Joaquin Valley. There was no stopping and starting in the empire building. It started in Healdsburg, got bigger and bigger, rolled like a snowball into San Francisco and kept on rolling.

CHAPTER 8

CENTRAL CALIFORNIA CANNERIES

After Joe got to the city, he accelerated his activity. Everything grew at a dizzying pace. Rather than try to record the activity year by year, this and future chapters will trace the history of each of the major enterprises. The largest operation was the canning business, with the usual humble beginnings in Healdsburg. The following chronicle was written by Robert M. Barthold, another of the wonderful managers that Joe was continually able to find for his businesses.

"The company started life as the Russian River Packing Company in 1890; later became Miller & Hotchkiss, and in 1901 was incorporated, under the laws of California, as the Central California Canneries. Its physical beginnings were at Healdsburg, California, in a little cannery operated by J.R. Miller. The cannery, in need of capital, was sort of limping along when William Josephus Hotchkiss, who had come from Kentucky to California and settled in Sonoma County, heard of its plight. He was a man of some financial means, and of a venturesome nature; and, after satisfying himself as to Miller's integrity and capability, he purchased a half interest in the cannery.

"With the needed capital, the Healdsburg plant made a creditable showing; and, during the next few years, Miller and Hotchkiss took over a plant at Sebastopol and several other small canneries- either under the name of Russian River Packing Company or Miller & Hotchkiss. These, also, did well, and their success prompted the organization, in 1901, of the Central California Canneries. The first listing of this concern was in the San Francisco Directory of 1902, as follows:

<u>Central California Canneries</u> (W.J Hotchkiss, Presdt. And Mngr., Robert M. Barthold, Accountant,) 123 California Street.
"In the next two directories the listing was the same, except that in 1904 their address had changed to 111 Front Street, and R.W Barthold had become Secretary. Their offices were burned out in the San Francisco disaster of April, 1906, but they soon found temporary quarters at 633 Howard Street. They were located there until 1908, when they moved to 1 Drumm Street, where they remained until the merger.

"For some years prior to 1906, Central operated a large cannery in San Francisco in what is now known as the North Beach area. The building had been erected by the California Wire Works, which made the cables for San Francisco's cable cars. When the wire company moved out, Central leased the building and installed canning equipment of the most modern type. It was here, and in a small cannery they operated in Emeryville, that Central's plant superintendents worked out and perfected the "lye method" of peeling peaches, which revolutionized peach canning, since previously this fruit had all been peeled by hand.

"Central's San Francisco cannery was destroyed by fire on April 18, 1906, but, contrary to the common experience, this fire was not caused by the earthquake. Instead, it was set by the plant engineer (later proved to be a pyromaniac), who after setting several other fires in San Francisco and one in Yuba City, was arrested, convicted and sent to San Quentin. The superintendent of this plant was a very capable man named Aitken, who, after the 1906 fire, went to Central's Emeryville cannery and later to the Yuba City cannery which Central operated for some years and then bought from the Armsbys in 1911.

"As of May, 1907, according to an article in a Pacific Coast canning journal, Central California Canneries was operating plants in Sacramento, Visalia, Sebastopol, Emeryville and San Lorenzo, and had selling and operating contracts with the Armsby Preserving Company at Yuba City, and Pacific Asparagus Company at Moorlands. Of these plants the article states, in part:

"The Sacramento Cannery is splendidly located for peaches, pears and grapes; receiving a large percentage of its peaches and pears by river steamer.

"The Visalia plant is located in the very finest section for canning peaches in the state of California, and receives all its fruits by team direct from the ranches. The company owns the control of a large fruit ranch and has intimate relations with another large fruit ranch; the product of these two orchards being sufficient to supply the cannery with its entire wants. The delivery of fruit direct from the orchard on short hauls by team enables the cannery to pack out from three to five cases more from a ton of fruit than a ton shipped by rail will pack out.

"The Sebastopol cannery is better located than any cannery in

California for the packing of small fruits- cherries of all varieties, blackberries, and raspberries- all of which are received by teams from the growers on short hauls.

"The Lorenzo cannery was equipped last year, for the packing of vegetables only. It is now being equipped for all kinds of fruit also. It is splendidly located for packing cherries of all varieties; also apricots, tomatoes and peas- all received direct from the growers on short hauls.

"The Armsby Preserving Company's plant at Yuba City is operated under contract by Central, who has an option to purchase it. (They did so in 1911). The Yuba City territory is especially noted for fine peaches and pears. It also produces plums freely, as well as excellent tomatoes, peas, etc.

"The Pacific Asparagus Company's plant at Moorland is operated by Central, under contract, for packing asparagus only; it being in the heart of the best asparagus district. This plant... is capable of packing 25 to 30 thousand cases, but with slight improvement can easily pack 50 to 60 thousand. Central now has contracts with growers, and lands of its own in asparagus, that within three years will furnish them with enough asparagus for 100,000 cases.

"The "large fruit ranch" mentioned in the paragraph concerning Central's Visalia plant, was the property of the Visalia Fruit and Land Company, a wholly owned subsidiary of Central California Canneries. It was acquired by them because it owned and operated a large peach orchard, and thus assured Central of a sufficient supply of peaches for canning.

"Hotchkiss was a man of many interests besides canning. Indeed, he was not a canner in the technical sense. Before the organization of the Central California Canneries, he left management of his canning interests to his partner, Miller, and after Central came into being, actual management of the company gravitated more and more to R.M Barthold, who was head of Central in everything but name.

"Among Hotchkiss' other interests were gold mining, timber lands and winemaking. He owned a winery at Trenton and had an interest in another near Folsom, California. He helped to organize and was later president of the California Winemakers' Corporation, of which

Herman Bendell of Tillman & Bendell was the first head. He had a part interest in several California and Nevada gold mines; and soon after the Klondike "strike" occurred, he and Miller set off for Alaska, leaving Barthold in full charge of the canneries."

Joe had so many interests that he could not get involved in too much of the details of the canning business. Bob Barthold proved himself to be capable, and Joe was happy to turn over more and more of the canning business to him. The unproved family legend says that Barthold was first hired as an office boy. Whatever the starting position, Joe would have been grateful for every rung up the ladder that Barthold could climb. Inevitably, the two would become good friends. Barthold went on to become President and later Chairman of the Board of Calpak.

Forty years later Joe's descendants were attempting to simplify the ownership of Visalia Orchard Company. They discovered that Barthold was the owner of one share and asked him if he wanted to sell it. He wrote a letter in response:

"Dear Mr. Hotchkiss, Your kind offer to dispose of my one share of the Visalia orchard Co. is appreciated.

"I located the certificate issued in April 1903 and found it signed by two of my dear friends, Carlton H. Wall and W.J. Hotchkiss. So as a matter of sentiment after holding it fifty years, I decided not to sell it at present."

Barthold had no first hand experience with the earliest history of the Miller and Hotchkiss operations, so he consolidated and simplified them. A fuller explanation is contained in the following excerpts from *Illustrated Atlas of Sonoma county, California (1898)*, published by Reynolds and Proctor:

THE RUSSIAN RIVER PACKING COMPANY
The growth of Immense Establishment of Miller & Hotchkiss.

"Sonoma County is by nature calculated, on account of its fertile soil and climatic conditions, to produce all varieties of deciduous fruits in perfection. Our thrifty population is ever progressive and ready to enlarge the field or our fruit production; but the producing of fruit is one thing and the successful and profitable marketing of it is another. Fortunately for Sonoma County active and energetic business men have given their energy, time and money to the developing of markets for our products. She has several large canneries within her boundaries, each of which will develop a market for its particular brand of fruits, and in turn offers to the grower that most necessary outlet for his products, a home market. Every fruit grower who has had any experience in marketing his fruits knows that when it is sent abroad to be marketed through the channels of trade, or through that most deceptive of all markets, the commission merchant, the returns are almost invariably disappointing, and in the end the results very unsatisfactory. On the other hand when a fair competitive home market is open to him at the point of production he is generally able to realize a fair profit on his investment and labor.

"Among the handlers of fruit, who offer to the Sonoma County fruit grower a market at the point of production, Miller & Hotchkiss rank first as the largest handlers of the raw material. Their cannery at Healdsburg is incorporated under the name of the Russian River Packing Company, and is one of the largest of the interior factories of the state. Situated in the midst of the producing district, in the fertile Russian River Valley, they are able to pack the fruits under the conditions most favorable for producing the highest quality of canned goods, for the best results can only be obtained in canning fruits where they are picked fresh from the orchards, being ripe and fully matured they have then their highest flavor, a condition impossible to secure where the fruits are picked green and allowed to ripen while being transported to market. This factory was established in 1891, and since its establishment its brands of goods have been steadily growing in favor on the markets until now its managers are able to dispose of their entire product, operating at its fullest capacity on all lines of fruit throughout the season. It is located near the depot of San Francisco and North Pacific Railway, and the various buildings cover more than an acre of ground lying along the railroad and connected with the main track by siding, which offers every convenience for the landing of fruit and shipping the manufactured product. The main building is 110x120 feet in dimensions, and adjoining are two warehouses, 72x120 feet. The machinery is all of the very latest manufacture, and the cannery plant is certainly one of the best managed and most efficient in the state.

"None but white labor is employed, and during the operating season from 500 to 600 hands are kept busy handling and preparing the luscious ripe fruits which come from the orchards immediately adjacent to the cannery. Neatness and cleanliness characterizes all of their work and their products are of the highest quality, impossible to equal by the large factories located in the larger cities.

"In addition to the cannery at Healdsburg the firm has a cannery of about equal size and capacity located at Sebastopol, also Sonoma County, a section noted for its fine fruits. The Sebastopol plant is operated under the same system as the Healdsburg plant. Both plants are of inestimable value to the fruit growers and give employment to much of the idle labor of Sonoma County, and are an equal blessing to the wage-earner.

"The product comprises all kinds of fruits, such as Bartlett pears, lemon cling, Muhr and Crawford peaches, plums, cherries, nectarines, etc. Owing to superior quality of the goods turned out by the firm the business has steadily increased until the entire output can be marketed. It is well located for packing a fine class of goods, and being close to the orchards the fruit is picked fresh from the trees, is placed in the cans without any delay while perfectly ripe, and thus the product possesses a flavor which cannot be excelled. The Healdsburg plant alone put up 40,000 cases of canned goods of 2,400 cans each, or nearly 1,000,000 cans requiring about 100 cars of 24,000 barrels each, representing 2,000,000 pounds of canned fruit, or 1,000 tons. The product of the cannery is all shipped to New York, Philadelphia and Boston.

"This firm makes a specialty of canning only extra quality of goods, and everything about the business is kept perfectly neat and clean, and all work is performed systematically. The fruit is all packed by white men and women, who are required to exercise care, that neatness and cleanliness shall characterize all their work.

"One broker, in commenting on the fruit put up by this firm, said 'that in every case where we have sent your goods out this year, we have received very complimentary letters about the quality.'

"The market for California fruit grows in direct ratio with the spread of knowledge concerning its merits. Consumers are learning that the long continued sunshine of California gives to fruit a flavor that cannot be secured in any climate where the presence of excessive moisture will not permit rays of the sun to do perfect work, nor irrigation advantages.

"The best and freshest fruit can only be packed by firms whose establishments are situated in the midst of orchards or near enough to them to insure the securing of fresh fruit, fully ripe. If fruit is picked before it is ripe the full flavor is not secured. If it is picked when fully ripe, and shipped any great distance, it becomes too ripe before it can be placed in the cans.

"With these facts in view the Russian River Packing Company located their cannery at Healdsburg, in the center of the great fruit growing section of Russian River and Dry Creek, and surrounding fruit orchards.

"The Russian River Packing Company is owned by J.R Miller and W.J Hotchkiss. It is located near the depot of the S.F and N.P Railway, and the various buildings cover more than an acre of ground lying along the railroad and connected with the main track by a siding, which affords every convenience for landing fruit and shipping the manufactured product.

"**Star Dried Fruit Company.** Messrs. Miller & Hotchkiss also do an extensive business in the drying of green and the marketing of dried fruits, under the name of the Star Dried Fruit Company. The buildings devoted to this industry are located on the opposite side of the railroad from the cannery and are equally well equipped. The drying grounds comprise about fifteen acres and require about twelve thousand trays.

"The drying season lasts ten or twelve weeks, and as high as two hundred hands are employed. Last season this firm shipped ninety cars of dried fruits, prunes, peaches and pears, to Eastern markets, representing 2,160,000 pounds of the dried article, or about 7,500,000 pounds of green fruit. Generally it takes from five to seven pounds of green peaches or pears to make one pound of dried fruit, and two and a half to two and three quarter pounds of green prunes to make one pound of dried fruit.

"The firm has done much to develop the dried fruit industry of Sonoma County and to educate the growers in the care and handling of their fruits, green and dried, so as to secure the best results in marketing.

"**The Wineries.** The firm of Miller and Hotchkiss also has two large wineries located one at Windsor and one at Trenton. These wineries are conducted for the best results, and none but the best wines are put upon the market.

"In the earlier stages of wine making in California ignorance as to the proper methods of production prevailed, and an inferior wine was the result, but ignorance has now given way to a knowledge gained by experience and a study of the processes used in Europe.

"The Windsor winery has a capacity of 900,000 gallons. In 1897 it crushed 4,000 tons, or 8,000,000 pounds of grapes and producing 600,000 gallons of wine. This winery has two filters and prepares its own wines for market. In 1897 the winery was run on the cooperative plan, the same as the wineries controlled by the California Wine Makers Corporation. The grape grower receiving $1.00 per ton for his grapes for each cent per gallon received for the wine.

"The Trenton winery has a capacity of 350,000 gallons and crushed in 1897 about 1,300 tons of grapes, making about 200,000 gallons of wine.

"In operating their great industries Miller & Hotchkiss employ only white labor and in the packing house and dryer give preference to such as can be drawn from Healdsburg and the immediate vicinity. Too much cannot be said in praise of the men who inaugurated and carry on these great home industries, which require a large amount of capital and great business sagacity."

It is wonderful how great you can look when you get to write your own material. Even with the gloss removed, the record is impressive. Miller and Hotchkiss had the advantage of access to Joe's cash hoard and borrowing power. He used the cash wisely to install the best and most modern machinery. Each plant was well located relative to the supply of fresh picked fruit. Joe's ability to choose and develop competent managers must have been legendary. Everything ran well, even with the limited amount of time that Joe could devote to any particular project.

Jim Miller was certainly a good manager. The record is not clear about when or why he left California to move to Seattle. It was most likely after Joe moved to San Francisco. The home industry became a much larger business, perhaps not to his liking. Also W.J. was getting into other businesses by himself. You can be sure of one thing. Jim Miller and Joe Hotchkiss parted as friends. Jim returned to the Bay Area many years later at the age of ninety. He had dinner with his namesake, James Miller Hotchkiss and had a wonderful time reminiscing about the good old days.

Jim Miller's place was taken by the next in line, Bob Barthold. Here was a man who could do an outstanding job running a cannery, a string of canneries and later a major corporation. He did it all for Central California Canneries and later for California Packing Corporation. He rose to prominence at the time W.J. was starting to stumble. Yet in his retirement he refused to sell a token stock certificate for one share because it had the signature of his good friend, W.J. Hotchkiss. That says a lot about both men.

CHAPTER 9

DEL MONTE

The canning industry in California started slowly and then accelerated dramatically. One hundred and forty-five thousand cases were canned in 1879. In 1899 the number had increased twenty fold to three million. The industry had its own timetable after the completion of the transcontinental railroad in 1869.

First came the passengers, accelerating to two hundred thousand a year, looking for a future in California. These people discovered that the fertile soil and beneficial climate were made to order for fruit and vegetable crops. Young trees were planted, and the fresh fruit boom was started.

Which came first, the fruit or the canneries? The answer is that the farmers needed the canners to provide a market. The canners needed the fruit as raw material for their operations. The farmers and the canners grew simultaneously.

The canners did not have a guaranteed profit. In fact disaster stared the smaller canners in the face at every turn. There was no concept of orderly marketing. The entire year's production was sold at the end of the canning period. Pricing was volatile. It was hard to find markets for the rapidly growing supply of fruit. The product was wonderful, but new consumers had to be convinced of this.

The unscrupulous canners were there also. They packed inferior fruit, put on a fancy label, and undersold their competitors. The effect on the marketplace was predictable. Pressure on the smaller canners was sufficient to encourage consolidation as a means of surviving. The *History of Del Monte* explained:

"In June, 1899 eighteen companies, comprising roughly half of the canning establishments in California, combined to form the California Fruit Canners Association (CFCA).

"The fact that CFCA, a stock corporation, chose to call itself an *association* provides an interesting insight into its organization and management style. Only a supreme optimist would have suggested that eighteen newly merged companies could be managed in other than a loosely decentralized manner.........Thus while CFCA was easily the leading factor in the California canning industry in its day, it never achieved the market dominance or the efficiencies of large scale production that would have resulted from the full integration of its considerable resources. One notable concession made to corporate solidarity was the adoption of the Del Monte label as the association's premier brand."

There were several major canners that did not join CFCA. Central was one of them. W.J. continued the good management and controlled growth for another seventeen years, while Bob Barthold played a more and more prominent role. Barthold described the marketing plan for Central:

"Central had three main avenues for the sale of its products. The first was through its own offices to Pacific Coast market areas. The second was through the Deming & Gould Company of Chicago and St. Louis, a large food brokerage firm which operated throughout the Middle West. The third was through the J.K. Armsby Company, who were sales agents for Central in all regions of the U.S.A not included in the territory of the Deming & Gould Co.

"Originally the Armsby Company had been sales agents for California Fruit Canners' Association. However, the Association decided to do all of its own selling and terminated the agreement with Armsby. Thereupon, the latter made a similar agreement with Central California Canneries, which continued up to the time of the Calpak merger.

"Sometime earlier the Central had made a sales agreement with Deming & Gould, covering regions of the Middle West; thereby establishing a business and personal relationship with Frank L. Deming, which grew closer over the years and culminated in his serving on Central's Board of Directors.

"As the Armsbys had lost California Fruit Canners' Association's business, and as they were rivals of Deming & Gould, they early sought to establish a close relationship with Central California Canneries. Shortly after entering into the sales contract arrangements with Central, previously mentioned, they began buying Central's capital stock, and ultimately built their holding up to about 45 per cent. At this time it became obvious to President Hotchkiss that they were seeking to gain control of Central; and although he was friendly with the two Armsby brothers (They were on Central's Board of Directors) and worked closely with them, he did not wish to lose control of the concern he had founded.

"Consequently Hotchkiss organized the North American Investment Company, as a holding company. This company then purchased sufficient of the non-Armsby stock in Central to give control, and made an agreement whereby none of this stock could be sold without the written consent of Hotchkiss."

The *History of Del Monte* Provides a colorful description of the Armsbys:

"Like many canning companies of the day, CFCCA initially sold most of its products through commission agents or brokers. For a time, its lead agent was a San Francisco based firm called the J.K Armsby Co.- the brokers J.K and G. for (George) N. Armsby, proprietors.

"Established in 1865 and originally headquartered in the Midwest, the Armsby company, by 1900, had become one of the largest wholesale grocery establishments on the West Coast. In addition to handling the CFCA line, it was exclusive agent for Alaska Packers Association. the leading canner of Pacific salmon, and did a thriving trade in western grown dried fruits and nuts as well. Old "Jake" Armsby, the founder of the company, had been a truly prodigious person: six feet seven inches tall and weighing over 300 pounds, with a personality to match his proportions. Booming, jovial, a man who enjoyed his pleasure and his work equally, he was the archetype 'traveling man' of his day.

"Physically and temperamentally, young J.K. was very much his father's son- a fine salesman and shrewd businessman who could quote the current market price of a hundred grocery items from memory. Brother George, on the other hand, had little interest in the mundane aspects of running a mercantile establishment. George's forte was finance. He was, in the words of a contemporary, 'a born deal-maker.'"

Did George put together a deal? Yes! It was what he once described as the merger of the best and strongest canners in the West, the General Motors of the canning industry. The newspaper headline screamed, "Canneries Of California In Great Merger". It had taken George a long time to convince each company that the deal was for their own good. Central California Canneries joined CFCA, JK Armsby

Company, Alaska Packers Association, and Griffin and Skelley Company to form California Packing Corporation (Calpak). Fifty years later the company name was changed to Del Monte, its leading brand name.

This was a merger of heavyweights. Bob Barthold provided enlightenment:

"As Griffen & Skelley were primarily dried fruit packers, the chief rivals in the canning field in California were the California Fruit Canners' Association and the Central California Canneries; and of the two, the latter seems to have been the better money-maker; due in part, no doubt, to the fact that it was a smaller, more closely-knit organization, and that all of its properties were productive. In any event, several years before the Calpak merger, the Central had built up a surplus greater than its capital stock, and in the year prior to the merger had net earnings of nearly $500,000.

"At the time of the merger Central had seven plants in operation-Sacramento, Yuba City, Rio Vista, Sebastopol, San Jose and Visalia, all of which became a part of Calpak after November 1916. When Central came into the merger, both President Hotchkiss and General Manager Barthold joined the Calpak organization, and both became members of its first Board of Directors. Hotchkiss was elected Vice President of the Corporation and Barthold was chosen as Sales Manager of the canned goods division."

By 1920 the Armsbys and Joe Hotchkiss had effectively retired from the new organization. Joe had too many other irons in the fire to look after. Bob Barthold stayed with the organization. He was appointed general sales manager in 1923 and president in 1930. He was later named chairman of the board and continued on the board for a total of forty-two years until his retirement. The Del Monte records note that Barthold was officially appointed general manager of Central in 1906 at the age of twenty-seven. We know that he was de facto manager before then. This great man may have been hired originally as Joe's office boy, but he didn't stay in that position very long.

CHAPTER 10

EVA BELL HITE, DOC WEAVER, NETTIE SNOOK AND CLEONE

"Wait a minute, wait a minute, stop the music!"

The often used cry of the great entertainer, Jimmy Durante, was used a century earlier by Emma Hotchkiss. Unlike Durante, Emma had no humor whatsoever. Preparations had been made in 1889 at the Hotchkiss ranch for the wedding of Eva Bell Hite. Rachel Miller, the next door neighbor, was practicing the wedding march on the organ when Emma's cry came. The wedding was off.

Emma lived in a simple world. Everybody fit into her individual hierarchy. In order of importance the categories were:

> Hite family relatives (Emma's mother was a Hite.)
> People from Augusta County, Virginia
> Southerners
> Democrats
> Emma's children
> W.J.
> Everybody else

Eva Bell fit the first four categories. She was Emma's second cousin, who had recently moved to California. She was also twenty years old and strikingly gorgeous. The wedding was a very special event for Emma. The records do not reveal the name of the loser nor anything about why the wedding was stopped.

Don't cry, Eva Bell, stay in Healdsburg for a while. Maybe your fortune will turn.

Charles Warren (Doc) Weaver was a licensed physician and a very close friend of W.J. and Emma. His family was well connected in Healdsburg. He eventually gave up his medical practice to become president of the local bank. Lorena Edrington said that Doc Weaver was a frequent visitor at the ranch, just as a visitor. He also responded to all of the family's illnesses. They were the only family that he continued to treat as a doctor. He was a thirty-five year old widower at the time.

Not surprisingly, Doc Weaver and Eva Bell Hite fell in love. Both of them were in the mood to get married. Rachel Miller was still out of a job as organist. The marriage was at the Presbyterian Church in Healdsburg. Tragically, the marriage ended in less than two years. The beautiful Eva Bell was dead from blood poisoning at the age of twenty-two. She is buried in the Weaver plot in the Oak Mound Cemetery in Healdsburg.

After W.J. moved to Berkeley, he returned many times for business and personal reasons. When he did not stay at the ranch, he stayed with Doc Weaver. Plans changed later when Doc took up with a lady from Cloverdale, who was a frequent visitor to Healdsburg on the weekends.

W.J. thought it was bad publicity for him to be associated with this sinning, so he switched to staying overnight with the widow Snook.

Could Emma possibly have believed this? "Emma, I'm very worried about staying with Doc Weaver in a house where sin is committed. I'm going to stay with Nettie Snook, where there is no sin." (so far).

Eighty years later Nettie's daughter, Cleone, told me, "Did you know that your grandfather was sweet on my mother?" I really didn't pay that much attention to the remark, but I was brought into direct contact with reality when Cleone emitted a definitive chuckle. There was no mistaking what this ninety year old lady had said.

Ed Snook was one of the many individuals who worked for Miller and Hotchkiss. He was a department manager, possibly also an investor. He separated from Nettie and moved out of the area, probably about the turn of the century. Ed's departure opened the door for W.J. There was no cash compensation to Nettie, who was very definitely a lady. Their infrequent liaisons were mutually rewarding. W.J. got the love and affection that he got in very limited doses at home. Nettie got the satisfaction of being the choice of a very wealthy and powerful man. It was also important to Nettie that she got the benefit of good business advice. She had money to invest. As a woman alone, she wanted to have support from W.J.

The personal gift from W.J. to Nettie was a beautiful strand of pearls. Nettie died in 1933 and left the pearls to Cleone, her only surviving child. With Cleone possession and honor sometimes battled.

She enjoyed possessing the pearls, but she thought the honorable thing to do was return them to the Hotchkiss family. For her the resolution came easily. She kept the pearls but told her confidantes that they should be returned to the Hotchkiss family after she died. It would have been a joy to me to own my grandfather's pearls, but reality set in. Nobody could find the pearls, so they slipped into history, to live only in this narrative.

Nettie Cole and her mother, Sarah Ann, were originally from Texas where Sarah Ann had raised eleven children on an isolated small farm. It did make a difference that the Cole family land holdings became part of the city of Dallas. Newly wealthy Sarah Ann was able to establish herself as a queen of Healdsburg society. Nettie married Ed Snook and established herself in the mausoleum business. She and Cleone are both buried in an incredibly beautiful mausoleum in Santa Rosa that was built by Nettie.

It would be impossible today to duplicate the elegance and quality of the edifice. It would cost more than one major fortune. Additional information on this interesting family is included in *Cleone Snook Stevens Tilley, Her Many Families* by James M. Hotchkiss, Jr.

Visalia Orchard Company was unique from its very beginnings in 1903. It was the only venture in which W.J. did not own a controlling interest from the beginning. The deal to establish a four hundred acre walnut ranch was put together by three good friends of W.J., with only roughly a one third interest taken by W.J. A few years later one of the principals died, and his widow wanted to be cashed out. The problem was that none of the remaining principals had any available cash at the time.

It was time for W.J. to put on his salesman hat. Regardless of whatever happened on the second floor, W.J. and Nettie conducted this business in the living room. Nettie agreed to buy the stock. Both of them agreed in writing that they would always vote their stock together, effectively exercising control of the company. Nettie became a director of the company, succeeded by Cleone and Cleone's husband, Russ Stevens. Cleone told me that she sat on the stairs eavesdropping at the age of eleven, when Nettie bought the stock. In later years Cleone and Russ traveled every year to San Francisco for the annual stockholders meeting. The meetings were simple and essentially a rubber stamp of what W.J. had done. In addition, Cleone followed in her mother's footsteps and gathered all of the financial advice that she could absorb.

W.J. became president of the company after Nettie bought the stock. The presidency was handed down like a British title to W.J.'s oldest son, J.M., and then to my older brother. I took over after my brother died. When I evaluated the company, I realized that it should be liquidated. All of the stockholders would be better off after liquidation. If I continued operations, I couldn't visualize a dividend return of more than two percent of liquidation value annually. All of the stockholders relied on the dividend income. They could get a substantially higher annual income by liquidating and investing the after tax proceeds in government bonds.

The problem was Cleone. After two thirds of a century you can develop an emotional attachment to a company. Would she be willing to liquidate? Cautiously and tentatively I tried to explain what I wanted to do. There was no need to worry. She said, "Jim, I think I've outgrown my investment."

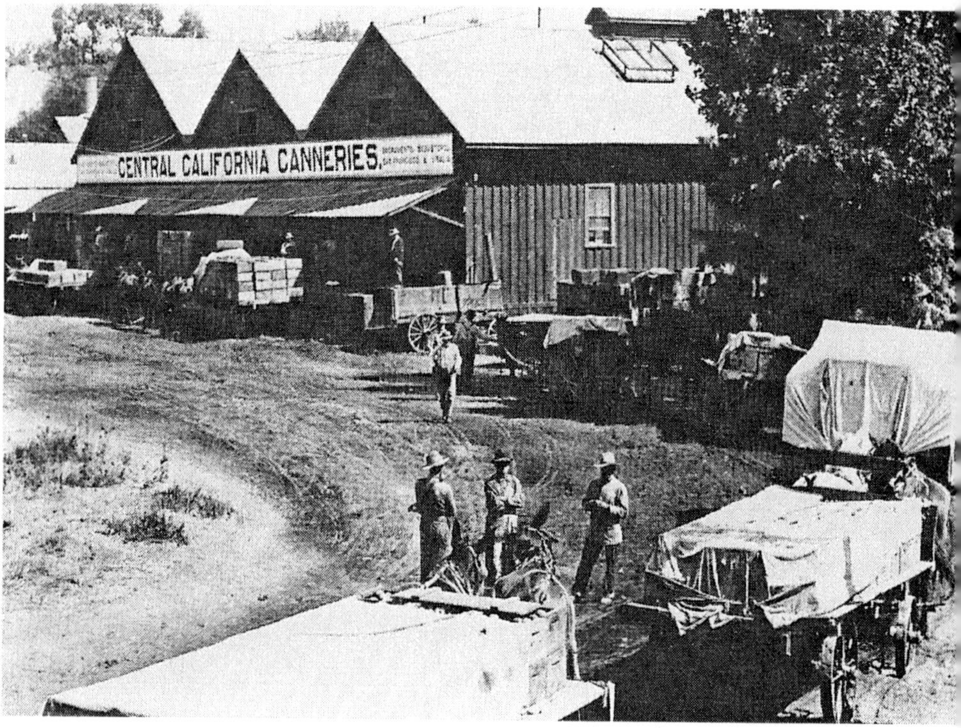
CENTRAL CALIFORNIA CANNERIES,

JAMES M. HOTCHKISS, JR. 65

Print Stone For Can Labels - (Central California Canneries)
Around the turn of the century (19th to 20th) flat stones like this one were used in printing colored labels (see sample label). The process was slow and arduous. It was eventually replaced by more modern methods.
Note the Hotchkiss "Glass jar" identification.

CALIFORNIA PACKING CORPORATION
101 CALIFORNIA STREET
SAN FRANCISCO

ROBERT M. BARTHOLD
CHAIRMAN OF THE BOARD

May 23, 1946

Mr. J.M. Hotchkiss, President
Visalia Orchard Company
1 Drumm Street
San Francisco, California

My dear Miller:

    Thank you for the report of the Visalia Orchard Co. The showing is excellent under the conditions existing this past year. My congratulations.

Sincerely yours,

RMB:hm

INFORMATION FOR SALESMEN

HOTCHKISS' "GLASS JAR" LABEL BRAND

CANNED FRUITS
AND
VEGETABLES

PUBLICATION Nº 486

CALIFORNIA PACKING CORPORATION
SAN FRANCISCO

One of the illustrations in "Information for Salesmen."
Note: Central California Canneries copyright at top of can.

Knightsen Santa Fe station 1915 Reported to be one of California's largest milk shipping centers.

THE MAIN SUPPORT

Reprinted from Editorial Page of the

San Francisco Examiner

of March 28, 1923

Knightsen ranch house Occupied by Marius Hotchkiss and family

72 A PAIR OF KINGS AND A JOKER

Del Norte County--"A While Back"

A head rig and workers used to saw raw logs as they come into the mill at Hobbs-Wall. Around 1900.

Emma enrolled her daughter, Hazel, and all the other relatives she could think of in the United Daughters of the Confederacy.

Sample Stock Certificate

Berkeley home of W. J. Hotchkiss from 1902 to death of both W. J. and Emma in 1936. The ten grandchildren always referred to it as the "big house".

In 1932 the shades in the cupola were opened wide. Four giant size poster portraits of presidential candidate Franklin Delano Roosevelt were hung for the whole world to see.

Other view of the "big house"

CHAPTER 11

MARIUS

Healdsburg, Calif.
December 13, 1890.

Dear Santa Claus,
    I wish you will please bring a viloscepede, a drum, a horn, some candy, a little wagon, that is by CMR Dugleys store. I would like you to please bring me a little wheel barrow. I want some peanuts, some oranges, bananas. I want a little whip. If you will please bring me a little gun that will shoot buck shot I will be very glad. I want a little sword. I will be so glad when Christmas comes, and I think we will have a nice time. Miss Hite is visiting us. I have three brothers and one sister.
        Your affectionate friend,
        Marius Hotchkiss

Marius was barely six years old when he took pencil in hand and wrote Santa. Outside of his spelling of velocipede, the letter is a very good example of sentence structure and vocabulary. It conveys the glorious Christmas enthusiasm of a very intelligent young man. A wonderful future was in store for Marius. What went wrong?

Emma and W.J. had produced four husky boys who competed against each other vigorously. There was no relief with sister Hazel, who was the most competitive of the bunch. They were all athletic, but Marius and Hazel had the most special skills. One big difference among the boys was the joy in telling stories on themselves. Marius never told stories about himself unless they were embellished with a few lies that helped aggrandize Marius. On the other hand, the other boys loved to tell their stories and do practical jokes.

Homer: Miller, why doesn't the car you sold me run?

Miller: That's the wrong question, Homer. The right question is why did I sell you the car, and the answer is because it doesn't run.

Undoubtedly, the story was at least partially true. However, Miller would have stopped short of really fleecing Homer. The importance of the event was in the story, not in the economics.

Once the boys hired a man to pose as the bearer of a neighborhood petition. Emma adored her cat, Blue Boy. She quickly signed the fake petition when she was told it was a request for the authorities to control all dogs that chase cats. The boys were ecstatic when they read out loud what Emma had signed, "Resolved that the authorities stop dogs from chasing cats by killing all the cats in the neighborhood."

The family lived on the ranch in Healdsburg until they moved to Berkeley. Emma was a strong disciplinarian. She had a lot of things to do, and she was not going to let any of her kids take her time away by misbehaving. Into the woodbox they would go, with no time allowed for argument or protest. She was respectfully addressed as "Mother" by her children. Only later, as grandchildren started coming, did her name change to "Gaga". Her daughters-in-law were scared to death of her. Her own children gave her their love and respect combined with a dose of fear.

All of the children except Marius managed to get along with Mother while they were growing up. Somewhere along the way Marius found that he could yell at his mother, and she would respond by yelling back at him. To Marius this was undoubtedly an improvement over being put in the woodbox. It gave him satisfaction to hear the response. In the future he would provoke a shouted response from his wife and his son as often as he could get away with it.

What saved the family from destruction by Marius was the collective sense of humor. W.J. loved a good joke. Although Gaga and Hazel were humorless, Marius' three brothers all had a keen sense of humor. In the third generation the sense of humor was inherited by most of the ten grandchildren of W.J., including Marius' son Miller. Even in the midst of a big fight with his father Miller could stop to laugh. Like magic, the anger would slip away.

The family had a bit of trouble differentiating between Marius' brother Miller and Marius' son Miller. They finally resolved the matter by referring to Marius' brother as big Miller or J.M. The next generation's Miller was called little Miller. Big Miller and all of his siblings had attended the Sotoyome School. Homer and big Miller had gone on to Healdsburg High School. Both excelled academically. Homer wanted to go to the University of California and pursue an education in engineering.

He didn't care that he was only fifteen years old in 1898. He had the necessary credits.

Big Miller liked Healdsburg and wanted to wait until he was eighteen before he moved to Berkeley. The mantle of the oldest son in the family was thrown over big Miller's shoulders. He was to go to Berkeley and watch over Homer.

The year 1898 was one of family change. Benoni died in May, and the two oldest boys went to college in Berkeley. The boys were certainly not abandoned. The family had many friends in the San Francisco Bay area, and it would be only a couple of years before the whole family moved to Berkeley, first to a rented house near the college campus, then a year later to W.J.'s final home at 2985 Claremont Avenue.

Homer and Miller were nearing the end of their college days. For the rest of the family it was new schools in the urban area. Hazel and Linville went to Berkeley High School. Someplace along the way Marius' academic career got sidetracked. He was probably playing semi-pro baseball in the Healdsburg area for a while. He finally surfaced at Lick, a prestigious college preparatory school in San Francisco, graduating in 1905 at the age of twenty-one. Lick later combined with Wilmerding and became the Lick Wilmerding school that still has a great reputation in San Francisco a hundred years later.

If you only looked at the photographs from that year, Marius was easily identified as the man you would least want to buy a used car from. He appeared scheming and shifty eyed. However, the written word was an entirely different story.

From *The Lick Tiger*, December 1904

"The [football] Team
Capt. Hotchkiss, who led the 1904 team to the championship of the Academic League, has proved himself to be one of the best prep. School centers of his weight that I have ever seen on the gridiron. He has all those qualities which go to make up a first class center; namely, speed, grit, brains and the "never-say-die spirit." His passing of the ball has been accurate and of the highest order. No captain could have set a better example to his team of hard work on the field, both in games and practice, than Hotchkiss did."

It took four lines in the commencement issue to list Marius' two years on the football team, the last year as captain, plus a year on the track team, two years on the baseball team, and three years on the tennis team. He was also the athletic editor of The Tiger and floor manager of the Christmas Dance.

It was a long way down from his career at Lick, but Marius managed it. His behavior was never so bad that anybody thought of drumming him out of the family, but he became mean spirited and totally capable of lying, cheating and stealing.

Marius' lies were created as appropriate to the situation. He was fully capable of creating a total story if necessary. More often, an embellishment would suffice. His car was hit many times by others, but it was never his fault. When he drove across the track in a railroad switching area, he was hit by an engine that was probably going less than one mile an hour. Marius was not hurt, but his front door was knocked off. The story was told like this, "I was driving along, minding my own business, when a big train came up out of a hole in the ground and hit me." Knowing enough to avoid ending on a basic lie, Marius added, "but the engineer was a nice fellow. He backed up the train and got some wire for me to fasten the door back on."

He could not find anybody in business to cheat. Actually he was easy prey for almost anybody in the business world. He found his cheating niche in cards. A family friend came one day to kibitz at a card game. Quietly, the kibitzer asked one of the players out of Marius' earshot, "Don't you know that Marius is cheating?"

"Oh yes," was the reply, "but he won't play with us unless we let him cheat."

It was hard for Marius to steal from anybody in business for the same reason that he couldn't cheat. He found that it was safe to steal from his dead father. He removed the ring from his father's hand. Then he gathered a crew from his ranch and moved much of the furniture from his father's home to Marius' home.

Living with his sense of humor rather than his anger, Miller wrote this delightful description of Marius in his 80's still lying routinely:

Why I Went To A Psychiatrist
(A short Play in three parts)

On May 1 East Side Ranch was billed by MWH for $612.20 covering purchases of miscellaneous surplus items.

On May 2 ESR issued check #1262 for the above amount to MWH and mailed same to 91 Hazel Road.

During the next two weeks MWH stated that he had not been paid and that if we had sent a check it had been lost, either in the mails or by Helena.

ON May 21 we wrote Crocker Anglo Bank asking them to notify us if the check had been paid or not.

On May 22 Crocker Anglo notified us that the check had not been paid.

On May 23rd we issued a stop payment order on the above check/

On May 24th we issued a check #1333 (lucky number) for the above amount to MWH and mailed same to 91 Hazel.

On June 4th we received the May bank statement. In it were:

#1262 deposited Elmwood Wells Fargo on May 6th. Signed M.W Hotchkiss

#1333 deposited Alameda Wells Fargo on May 29th. Signed Marius W Hotchkiss and Thomas W. Swain.

On June 10th the matter was personally taken up with MWH. He said it wasn't so. He was presented with the two checks, he studied them, he was speechless. One hour later he explained to me how it happened.

1-#1262 was opened by HBH who deposited it and forgot to: mention it, enter it in the checkbook, keep the deposit slip. (there is no explanation of how the check came to be endorsed by MWH in his writing.)

2- #1333 was different. He (MWH) is handling things slightly different now but it was all written into the check book so there is a record. The Mormon Church wanted their money ($500) right now and he didn't have a check with him so he gave them the #1333 check which he just happened to have with him. The Mormon Church (alias Tom Swain) gave him a check for the difference $112.20 and he deposited this in the bank.

Extras: (for free) Swain called him up yesterday and told him to come and get his money ($500) which he is going to do right away.

He bought three locomotives (I assume these are the old kind that have boilers on them) for $875 and he had gotten his money back already from one of them and has made a deal with a man (on the side of a hill) to scrap out the 160 tons and split the profit. However he is keeping the wheels underneath as another man told him he should get $6,000.00 for these.

When you buy a locomotive, is your motive loco?

In his narrative Miller slyly inserted a couple of current references to Marius' recent activities. He was into buying very large pieces of equipment and then scrapping them (almost always without profit).

He had a special attraction to large boilers, hence the reference to boilers on locomotives. It was about this time that Miller's ranch had a visitor from the border inspector, looking for illegal aliens. It took Miller a while to get to his own world. For the first half hour, he believed that he was talking to the boiler inspector.

A rather interesting trait ran in the Hotchkiss family. Marius and his brothers had very poor memories for names of individuals. Marius compounded the problem by mispronouncing the names that he tried to say. The local baseball team had a pitcher named Tom Ananicz (rhymes with bananas). Marius called him Ananickease or Anarack. The biggest blunder was the great baseball player, Orlando Cepeda. Marius never changed. He always called him Potato.

In business Marius wandered freely in the black and Japanese communities. Like his sister, he showed no prejudice of any kind. However, he was not going to get caught mangling the names. He was happy to proclaim that he had made a deal with the Jap in Capitola. He could easily be distinguished from the Jap in Berkeley or the Jap in Stockton.

Sometimes people were identified by a physical characteristic. There was the guy with a limp, also the Indian truck driver. This last guy had a very short name, Bill Igo. Marius took a chance and often called him by name, but it always came out Immy.

When Marius actually got a noun into his memory bank, it stayed there forever. Many members of his generation used the word "central" to describe a telephone operator in the early days of telephone service. Only a few people retained it to their death. Marius was one of them. He was the same way with the word "machine" to describe an automobile. In farming, people used the word "grass" to describe the asparagus that they grew. The word went out of favor with everybody except Marius. He ate grass to the end.

Miller's absolute favorite was the ultimate climax of Marius' way of identifying people. Marius told Miller that he had made a deal with "the two guys on the hill". From this came Miller's wry comment about a man on the side of the hill.

I spent a lot of time trying to keep track of Marius' business dealings and trying to prepare income tax returns for him. One time Miller and Marius and I had a short conference:

Miller: Marius, you are losing money all the time with this junk business of yours.

Marius: No. I know how to do these things. I always make money.

Miller: But Marius, it shows on the income tax returns. Every year you lose money.

Marius: Jim just does that to save on income taxes.

Miller: [Speechless]

Jim: [Speechless]

Was Marius unclear on the concept or was he simply ignoring

anything that got in the way of his world? Eva Lee Calhoun once wrote a letter to Miller:

"Marius wanted to go to Ukiah next Tuesday and leave Helena and me at my sister's in Healdsburg. I phoned him and said that I would cancel my hair appointment but he was not to leave us stranded for six hours in Healdsburg. He said, 'What do you mean? You can sit just as well there as you can at home.'

"I said it is not easy to make small talk and try to be social for six hours. Just now he phoned me and said we will go next week. He just does not comprehend!"

Marius was surprisingly well adept at the big lie or a long string of half truths. It was a family trait. In his retirement, brother Linville traveled the world. Everywhere he went he was happy to tell anybody who would listen that he owned the world's largest stamp collection. He also said he owned Rudolph Valentino's bed.

One time Marius and Helena in their cross country travels visited Campbellsville, Kentucky, the birthplace of Marius' father.

Soon Marius found his way to the local newspaper office. This was the perfect venue for Marius, an open window to tell half truths and exaggerate without limit. No one in town had enough knowledge about W.J. and his operations to call Marius a liar. Here are excerpts from the newspaper article of April 11, 1946, followed by the real truth:

County Pioneer Heirs Farm Huge Estate

"Last week, Campbellsville had for its visitor, one of California's great farmers, Mr. Marius W. Hotchkiss, of Berkeley, Calif., accompanied by his lovely wife, for a visit of a few days to his cousin, Mrs. J.P. Gozder and Mr. Gozder.

"Mr. Hotchkiss is a grandson of an early pioneer family of our city, whose grandparents, Mr. And Mrs. Benoni Hotchkiss left Campbellsville in the early '49 for the great West to make their home in the Golden state." [Nice try, Marius. These were not 49ers. They left in 1859.]

"As the story is told to us by our visitor, his grandparents with their son, Will Joe, left here in a covered wagon, and after a six month's trek thru the states into California, they arrived at Woodland, Calif., where Mr. Benoni bought a Spanish grant of land in Sonoma County, consisting of 1400 acres for the price of $400. he farmed at night, taught school in the daytime, and his wife operated a boarding house. In after years Will Joe took over the management of this acreage, which had grown and known today as the Hotchkiss Estate Corporation, farming more than twenty-eight thousand acres of land in and near where the original purchase was made by his father, Benoni."

Is there anybody out there who can farm 1400 acres at night? Marius is doing a systematic removal of Barrett Edrington from the Hotchkiss family history. The farm was Barrett's, probably much less than 1400 acres. Benoni built the hotel in Woodland, and then moved to the Healdsburg ranch of 375 acres. At the height of his empire W.J. held throughout California considerably less than the 28,000 acres that Marius claimed.

Always sloppy with the details, Marius was quoted as saying W.J. died six months before Emma instead of afterward. W.J. was an early pioneer in the San Joaquin Valley, but he certainly was not the first to dig a well or plant cotton there. Many farmers wanted the Mendota dam. W.J. did not build it. He did not establish the first canning plant in Central California. He did not even have the first cannery in Healdsburg. Marius himself owned only one half of, not the entire Cheek and Hotchkiss ranch. He described how he operated the ranch, ignoring the fact that it was managed by his son. Miller would not even let Marius come near the ranch. Marius went on and on, giving the reporter one half truth after another.

On the other hand, Marius had no reason to lie about the German prisoners of war. His is the only family account of this operation, and he deserves credit for preserving the information. The Campbellsville paper included all this in its article:

"During the recent war [World War II] the Hotchkiss estate worked 750 German prisoners who were guarded and managed by American officers. They were housed in the Hotchkiss Camp, which is an immense building, large enough for 1000 people. The mess hall is massive and the cooking stoves in the kitchen are 40 feet long. The Estate Corp. paid to the government for the use of the Germans $7.50 per day, and they in turn received from our government 80 cents per day for their labor including board. Those German employees who did not obey orders or did not do their work right, were placed into prison house on dry bread and water for 14 days. After serving this sentence and going back to work, and still not obeying or doing their work right, would be slapped back into prison house for another 14 days. And those prisoners who did perform and work right, ending their stay in camp without black marks, our government paid them $300.00 cash, as a premium for good behavior. All around the camp, Guard towers were built and 35 guards were constantly on the watch. All prisoners were required to hang their shoes on the picket fence, and walked into those houses in bare feet. These prisoners came out of the African theatre of war."

CHAPTER 12

MARIUS AND THE LUMBER BUSINESS

W.J. got his start in the lumber business in 1902. The following paragraphs are excerpted from Successful American, February, 1904:

"In September, 1902, together with some business associates, Mr. Hotchkiss purchased the firm and business of Hobbs, Wall & Co., of San Francisco, together with lumber mills in Del Norte County, large holdings, of redwood and pine timber, wharves, vessels for the transportation of lumber and the principal box factory in San Francisco. The deal involved $1,500,000. This enterprise has been most successful, and has encouraged Mr. Hotchkiss and his associates to embark in other large enterprises in the same line. Recently, the Simpson Lumber Company's mills, timber lands, railroads and wharves, which practically adjoined the Hobbs, Wall Company property in Del Norte County, was purchased, and is now operated in conjunction with the Hobbs, Wall Company.

"Another venture of Mr. Hotchkiss which, like his other ones, is a marked success, was the purchase of the Port Blakely Milling Company. This property includes the valuable Washington Pine and Cedar Timber Land, amounting to 78,000 acres, which is one of the largest individual holdings on the Pacific Coast. Besides this, the Company owns and operates the largest lumber mill in the world, at Fort Blakely, Washington, which has an output of over ten million feet of lumber a month."

W.J. could manage the business from San Francisco, although it was a big business and needed a lot of managing. The main center of lumbering was Crescent City in Del Norte County, at the extreme north of the State of California. W.J. made frequent trips by ship to keep track of things. As usual, he had managed to find a very competent site manager in George Keller. One letter from Keller has been preserved. It is a masterpiece of comic overtones applied to a business report:

The forescent City.

The ladies of the W.C.T.U. called upon me and asked to have

H.W. + Co., cooperate with them in their movement. I asked them what their plans were, and they had none whatever, except that they wanted to do good for the Community and people in general. The counciltation wound up by H.W. & Co. donating some cups-and saucers and some chairs for their rooms, but we expect to cooperate with them and help on any just lines wherever we can. They asked me if I had any suggestions to offer and I advised that they try and legislate to have the saloons closed up at 11 o' clock each night and on Sundays, and I think if they accomplish this, it would be a long way toward reform in Crescent City. Furthermore I knew it would be to our benefit if they could get things regulated in this respect.

Yours truly,
Hobbs, Wall & Co.
Per------------

The coined word "counciltation" is perfect for the letter. It is probably not the first time that George used "forescent City". That seems to be a nifty combination of forest and crescent.

The trip by ship from San Francisco to Crescent City was very rough, almost four hundred miles, and the lumber ship was slow. The ocean at Crescent City was mean and unforgiving. W.J. did what was necessary, but he was happy when his sons developed and were able to take over some management responsibility, especially the trip by ship. As the oldest son, J.M. (big Miller) took on the greater share of responsibility. He was a natural businessman with ventures of his own, but he also worked for W.J. and Hobbs Wall.

An anecdote about J.M. is worth telling here. He had terrible handwriting. One day his secretary was sick, so he wrote a letter by hand to George Keller. When the letter arrived, George could not read it, nor could anybody in his office. It was not treated as a disaster, because they knew J.M. was scheduled to arrive by ship two days later. Inevitably, J.M. arrived, but he couldn't read the letter either.

W.J.'s second son, Homer, graduated from the University of California with a degree in engineering. He was also sent to Crescent City, where he picked a wife, Edna McVay, but he showed no great love for the lumber business. The boy who came down to college at the age of fifteen later went to South Africa to work as an engineer in a gold mine. While there he acquired an illness that would take his life at the age of forty-one.

There is also an anecdote about Homer that is worth repeating. It sounds terrible, but there was unquestionably a twinkle in W.J.'s eye when he said about Homer, "All that money I spent for his college education, and he couldn't even build me a railroad one mile into the woods."

The third son was Marius, who was almost twenty-one when he graduated from Lick High School in 2005. Two relatively unsuccessful years at the University of California followed. Nobody knows whether W.J. was still expecting great things from Marius. Hope springs eternal. We do know that Marius was living in Crescent City in the home of George Keller in the fall of 1907. Nobody ever mentioned if George was happy with the plan or if he was bribed with a hefty salary increase.

History has a habit of repeating itself within families. Thirty-two years later J.M.'s oldest son, Bill, had two undistinguished years in college, which he followed by eloping at the age of twenty. He had no job and no prospects. J.M. rewarded this precipitate behavior with a job at the family ranch in the middle of nowhere near Firebaugh, California. Happily, that one turned out well. Bill learned to work hard, and his wife came to light as a shining jewel in the family.

In 1907 Marius met Helena Crusius. Helena was much more than a simple country peasant. She was the daughter of the County Treasurer. It was acceptable that she should meet Marius. It was also acceptable that Helena would be sent to Oakland, California, to attend the fashionable Snell Seminary, which was also attended later by her sister Lillian. Happily for historians, Marius wrote Helena there eleven times, plus another ten letters after she moved to San Francisco. Helena preserved the letters, which were discovered after her death. The earlier letters include material relating to Hobbs Wall and small town life in that era. The story of developing romance is in the following chapter. Helena was not quite eighteen years old when the letters started. Marius was five years older. Frequently mentioned in the letters are Helena's four younger sisters, Lillian, Fran, Edna and Gertrude.

Crescent City, Ca
September 23, 1907

My dearest Girl,

Well dear I have not had any time to write to you before and really have not time to write now, but will take time. I am afraid that this letter will have to be pretty short as my supply of news is limited.

I received your letter Sunday, and would have answered it then but my hands were so sore from pulling rigging and by having Brads stuck into them that they were in no condition to write.

I think George carried the letter around in his pocket for a while before I got it. I wonder if you will write to me before you receive this letter I bet you will not for you are just that contrary (I am afraid dear.) We had a fine trip up on the boat, it was very calm.

George had a big bunch of Indians to see him last night. To see what he was going to do about the digger the train killed. One digger cut a squaw today and the diggers are very excited. Mrs. K had not come home yet. We wrote her a very blue letter yesterday telling her that George had taken a little Indian to raise, one of the children of Andrew George, the Indian that was killed. Al said in the letter that Mrs. K had to come right home. As it was bad enough before, but since the little digger had come that it was the limit. All she could get out of George was we will get lots of Indian baskets now. She said that she told him that Mrs. K would not have the Indian in the house. When she came home and that George said she would have to keep trim. We also said that he was very dirty but cute. In fact it was a grand letter all the way through. We are going to tell the stage driver to tell Mrs. K all about the kid so I guess she will expect to see a little Indian when she arrives home.

I would like very much to see my face and hope my face would like to see me. Your mother has treated us like Kings, we have lived like Kings. With lots of love for my dearest fair, fat and frivolous girl,

As ever yours, Marius

Crescent City
October 11, 1907

My dearest girl,

I have treated you very bad girl, in not writing to you sooner but found it very hard to find time. I think a good deal more of my future than I ever did, and wish she was here. I will write to you as often as I can and want you to do the same. I know I can trust you and will have no cause to call you a false any more.

I heard last night that Jessie C. and Paul were going to be married. Andrew is not going so much with Nell. I went to the prize fight last night, and it was very good.

Dear, this letter can not be very long, as I want it to go on tonight's mail.

The whole Keller family went to Smith River today.

My brother has started home from Africa, so I will see you in the course of a month or so. I will come down to see him when he gets home.

We had a big rough house up at Doktor's the other night. I put five through a window but did not hurt much but the window. We expect my father up in a few days. Today is a fine day. There is no wind to speak of, and the sun is very warm.

I am writing this letter in a great hurry dear but hope you can read it.

Lillie is getting as big as you are, and you know how big that is. If you don't, I do.

With lots of love, yours, Marius

Crescent City, California
October 29, 1907

My dear girl,

    Dear I have not had time to write to you for a long time, but you have not written to me either. You know my father has been up here and I have been with him a great deal. I also have been down to Eureka, so you see dear I have not had much time. George, my father & yours truly were lost in the woods the other night. We went 24 hours without any thing to eat, we were wet to the skin from contact with the wet bush. We had no matches, so we had to stay and freeze all night. After this dear I will try to be better about writing to you and hope you will do the same. They want me to take part in a church play, but I told them that I was too busy. Some lady was saying the other day that it was strange that it took you so long to go through school, while all the others that had gone down from here, had finished so much sooner. Mrs. K is going to have the new house right away. She says she will not growl for a whole year.

    I was out duck hunting yesterday and the automobile broke down, It sounded like hell. I was wet through the skin, but we killed lots of ducks.

    Nell Jones is in the telephone office. Hinie will be down in a week or two. You must be getting lazy for I have not heard form you for a long time. If you don't hear from me you should write any way dear, because I like to hear from you.

    I have a map to draw so will close with lots of love as ever
Yours dear,
Marius

October 30, 1907

My dear girl Helena,

    I received two letters from you today dear. One dated the 21 and the other the 29, that is the date on the post mark. I just got back from hunting ducks and as I got up at 5 o'clock this morning I am a little sleepy. I don't see where your letter could have been. Henry is coming down on the next Delmont so you had better be on your best behavior.

Last night Alec Smith ran into a door and hurt himself, nothing serious, only marred his beauty for the time being.

I want you to be sure and keep your promise to me dear, that you would write and let me know when I am cut out.

I guess when you come back from the city, Mrs. K will have her new house.

My brother will be home the fifteenth but I do not know whether I will come down then to see him or wait till I go down Christmas.

You go to all the parties with Edd don't you?

You should see my hands the way they are scratched up from the night in the woods. My father thinks Lillie looks just like you, I told him that in facial features there was a great similarity, but in figure that you would make two of Lillie.

Your last letter dear was pretty cold, it kind of looked as if you were getting thick with Edd again.

Alice has the Oregon fever so she is going back to Oregon to try to get married. Somebody said to me the other day, "Mrs. K is not over 85 is she!!" Well dear I will close with lots of love,
Yours Marius William Hotchkiss.

Crescent City,
November 6, 1907

My Dear Girl,

I wrote you a letter four or five days ago and left it up at the house to be mailed and I found it there yesterday still unmailed. So I mailed it last night.

Hinie is coming down on the Delmont to stay three weeks. The wreck is still on the rocks and I guess will be there for quite a while if the storms do not break it up.

Dr. Demorten is still out at Smith River. I think he is trying to shake Nell but it is a pretty hard job I think Slats or Nell is working in the telephone office.

I had a letter from my mother wanting me to come down soon. George is looking badly. I think he is worried about the banks. I was out hunting Sunday and killed a lot of birds. The new M. preacher is supposed to be on this boat.

The Delmont is laying outside, it is too rough for her to land her passengers. Tagert shot Willie Murphy Saturday but did not hurt him much.

Dock is back working in the store. Joe Miller got fired for talking back to Edwards. I think he was just waiting for an excuse to give Joe his time. Alice gets very mad when we josh her about Joe.

Joe told every body that he quit, so when Alice came home and told us Joe had quit we told her that he got fired and she got pretty sore when we asked him if there was any danger of her quitting like Joe did. Well dear I can't think of any more to say so I will close with love.
As ever yours,
Marius

November 22, 1907

My Dear Girl,

I received your letter this evening and as I have a little time dear, I will answer it while I have the time. Mrs. K and Lena were reading a letter from you when I got home and their letter was longer than mine. You sealed Lena's letter and did not seal mine. Therefore hers must have been more important. You did not even mention the new blue dress.

We have lots of fun joshing with Fran. Fran has a new coat and Lillie has, like your self a new hat. So whenever we see them we take special notice of the fact, which makes them feel cheap.

Myrtle Jones has a new string to her bow. There is a new drummer in town.

You asked me dear why I thought Dock D. was trying to shake Nell. Well, he never stays up at the house at evening like he used to but comes downtown and stays pretty late.

Tonight for an example I walked up from the post office with him, it was about 5 minutes until nine. Nell was standing in the doorway with her hat and gloves on waiting for nine to come so she could go home. Dock did not wait but went right home. It looks as if he had cared any he could have waited five minutes to take her home. The store was short handed, so I drove the wagon for a while. I don't think many of the people recognized me with the flour and other stuff over my clothes and thought I was a thing to give the devil to. They would say, "why didn't you deliver so and so? I added it a week ago" and etc. It generally would turn out that they had or did it the day before after the wagon had gone to the barn. It seemed that everybody wanted wheat while I was on the wagon. You know that wheat only weighs about 150 lbs and by the time you have packed the sack around the house a couple of times, waiting for them to decided where they want it put, you know you have been doing something.

Your mother seems to have thrown off on us she does not send us anymore, good things to eat.

I guess you have heard that Joe Miller has left C.C. and departed for Eureka. We have not become reconciled to the loss yet. We try to josh Alice about it but she gets so mad we do not dare say more.

I have played baseball at St. Mathews a few times. We could always beat them very easily. I guess you have seen Hinie by now. I heard tonight that Mrs. Snider was going to marry Mr. Baird. I don't think there is any other news. Manly came up to me last Sunday and asked me if it was so that George was going to leave in a few days and I was going to take charge. I was out hunting the other day and could not shoot very well. I have been looking for jewelry for the store. You know they send us a lot from the city to select from. I just asked Alice what the news from the Eureka was, and I don't think she liked it very well.

Lillie says that the new hat is the first thing that she ever had that she could call her own.

Well dear as I have not a great deal of space left, I am afraid that I will have to close. Give my best regards to Henry if you should see him again. I wrote very small so this letter is very long.

With lots of love for my girl Helena,
Marius

November 25, 1907

As I have the time dear I will drop you a few lines. I am afraid it will have to be a very few as I know no new news. You of course knew that Else Ward had a fellow, so she says. She caught him while she was down below. He has light wavy hair and works for the telephone company.

Miss Big Lena licks Tony the little boy from the Miller Ranch nearly every day. Henry sent her a card with a picture of a woman licking the devil out of a kid and had the kid named Tony.

I made Lena think that Wolf told every body about it in town. And she was going down and give him a piece of her mind.

Quite a few C.C. people are coming down on the next Delmont leaving here Wednesday. Mr. Hamilton, wife and sister, Mrs. Stovers and some of the clients are among the bunch. When you come back up here, you will have to join Ethel and Violet in the WCTU.

We are thinking seriously of sending Alice and Big Lena down to the city to see if they will have as much success as Elsie did. We are going to have to do something pretty soon or it will be too late. George and I are thinking of advertising in the Heart and Hand for them. We are thinking of also adding Martha's C. name.

Today has been wet and cold. I wished you had been here so I could have seen you as I wanted to see you very much. Well dear I can not think of any more to say so I will close with lots of love for my dear girl, as ever yours,
Marius

There were no more letters in 1907. The holiday period was probably the reason. Up to this point, the letters have been accounts of life in a small town with some teasing thrown in. The teasing was sometimes barbed, but it was within tolerance. It is perhaps prophetic to note that teasing was slowly declining. Also, Marius addressed his dear girl as Helena in two separate letters, proving that he did know what her name was. In later years he angered her by always calling her Helen. How could he have forgotten?

Crescent City
February 27, 1908

My dearest Helena,

I received your pleasant letter in which you blew me up for not writing. I guess by now you have received two letters from me, so I will expect your apology before hand. You see I got in here one morning and left the next morning for parts unknown. The first night I assumed you could not expect me to write dear, as I was too tired after coming off the boat after the terrible trip we had. But as soon as I got back from my trip I wrote you a new letter. I left the first letter I wrote you here with Mrs. K., and maybe she did not mail it right away. We had a little excitement last night, the night five men went crazy and blew the fire whistle, and of course everybody thought that the mill was on fire.

You did not say dear who you had a chance to go riding with dear. I still think dear that you had four dances with our mutual friend that night. I am sure that you told me that you had. Your mother tells me that you will be out of school in a few weeks. How long are you going to stay before you come home?

Your mother has been very good to us lately and sent us lots of things. I saw Nell and Andrew the other night. They looked fine. I have had three very nice letters from you dear and have been very glad to get them. The household still remains in peace.

George and I are not going to Eureka until next week. Your mother and Miss A. was up this evening for a while. Mrs. K. went to a card party last night and won a prize. We are very proud of her, don't you wish you was as clever? When I was down to your house the other evening, Mrs. A. tried to josh me about you. She wanted to know about this sudden desire of yours to learn to cook and various other things, but I think I got the best of her in the long run.

I hope you are not getting fat as I am getting thin. The Delmont will be here tomorrow. The library is going to give a dance and supper the twentieth. I don't suppose you will be home by that time. The dump at mill two broke today and put a couple of men into the pond, but nobody got hurt. With lots of love for the dearest girl. Yours, Marius

March 22, 1908

Dear Girl,

    I am going out in the timber with the timber C. and may be gone for a week or so. So don't be alarmed if you don't hear from me. We had a terrible way up. The roughest in years. Every body stood it pretty well. I leave in a minute so can not write much. Your mother told me that your father said, "I guess it will be home soon as Marius is here now." With lots of love for my dearest girl,
Marius H.

CHAPTER 13

MARIUS AND HELENA

What a difference a day makes. The first letter in this chapter was written one day later than the previous one. The romance definitely escalated. The letters from now on relate repeatedly to love and marriage. After April fourth, Helena moved to San Francisco, but the letters continued.

Marius wrote ten times in April and twice more in May. Only the most interesting paragraphs are repeated here as if it was all a single letter. After the great revelation in the letter of March 23rd, Marius changed. His insecurities seemed to surface, and the teasing became bitter. It was perhaps all very confusing to an eighteen year old girl.

Crescent City,
March 23, 1908

My dearest Girl

I miss you a lot dear. I would lay awake nights and think about you, while with the Crugers. I have thought a lot about you wondering what you were doing and many other things lots nicer. I found some old letters you had written me which I read over a good many times. The nicest letter you ever wrote me dear was the one that you wrote a short time before I came down the last time. One of the letters in my old coat was a letter you had written me just before you had come home. It was a very nice letter. In one way it made me not mad dear but very sour balled. Not that I did not trust you more but it just did. I know it is a thing of the past and I should not mind it but I could not help feeling bad just the same.

I have thought more about you dear than I ever have before. I think I care more for you now than I ever have and you know how much that must be, don't you dear. The letter I wrote you the other day was written in five seconds as the men were waiting for me. I had no idea that I was going with them then that I could fly but G came along and told me I had better go with them so I did not have much time to write you. Yes dear I have been down to see mother in law and I think I will go again in a day or two. That is the first evening I am not too lazy to dress.

I am going to Eureka with George Saturday. Mrs. K says that as you will be home so soon she will not write you as you would have to answer it and that you are a very busy girl. There is a great well house up at K now. We have napkins and are served instead of reaching for what we want. We have many fancy dishes. G and I were alone in the dining room tonight and they brought me some potatoes and he said to me what in Hell is that, but they did not hear him. We are afraid that M will spoil Mrs. K she says we should not have much desert so we have not had any for three days. So G says I get up at 9 o'clock nearly as lazy as you dear isn't she.

George says she is too dam positive of everything she says. She told some thing at the dinner table and then I told a story about a fellow dropping a stone in a hole and hearing it hit after two days. She got mad and said that thing could be verified. Well dearest girl, I will write again soon for you are the dearest girl in the world,
Marius

Crescent City,
April - May 1908

My Dearest Girl,

When are you coming home dear? I will tell you dear what they did to Andrew, when you come home dear. And I guess you will see some of the disadvantages of getting married in Crescent City. I was down to see mother the night before last. I think marriage has improved Nell a lot. I wonder if it will improve you as much, for if it does you will be awfully nice.

We fooled some fellows on a cake today. The cook at Camp five made us a tallow cake and fixed it fine. Some of the boys at camp 6 swiped it, but when they started to eat it they found to their sorrow that it was tallow.

Lena looks fine in her new hat and brown dress. I suppose you have gotten your new hat by now. Mrs. Houston has been away for over a week, so we have been living in peace. Mrs. H has a very bad dose of poison oak.

Well dear as I have a few moments I will drop you a line. Letters from you do not come as frequent as they did when I first got home. Hinie and I were up to call on Andrew last night. I think they get along very well dear better than we will as Nell has such a nice deposition. Dock gives her $8.50 a month to do the washing. He gets up and gets breakfast most of the time (how foolish) do you think so dear? Dock also helps her wash the dishes. I think he will get over it, don't you? Be sure and bring Lena the box of candy she won off of you about Lilian never going to Paris after she had worked so long.

Joe Wall is working good, he got a nose broke the other day but working still. He does not draw much of his salary and the boys tease him about getting a wedding stake. We were down to see mother in law last night. She wanted us to go out and get some beer she said she was dry. She made some bad breaks. You should have been there to hear them. We all nearly died a laughing. We all went to the show the other night it was fun. Three killed in one act, I will send program.

I can only write you a few lines as Mrs. K wants me to go down and see your mother. I will write you a nice long letter tomorrow. My mother says for you to come out to the house dear. We had a train wreck this afternoon. We ran over a cow it ditched the train and was very disastrous to the cow.

I suppose you will be home some time next year. I received a letter from you last night which I did not get till this morning which was about time. For I had not heard from you for nearly a week. I am so sorry you were too sick to go to Snells, but were able to go to Mill Valley. Who was the fellow you went with, a new kill? I suppose you are getting to be a past master of flirting; you are having so many chances to practice.

The city election comes off tomorrow and I guess the WCTU will be out in full force. Mrs. K informed us this morning that she was going to have a cook. I guess we will have to get a butler and a valet for George, the next thing we know. I didn't wonder about you going home with Wilma. Are you sure the tooth ache was real or only a bluff. You say you always give in to me, well I'm glad to know it.

The flu makes a fine excuse don't it. What you are going to do, well I would say visit all your girl friends that have brothers. As far as your industry goes I'm sufficiently informed on that subject already. You made a little oversight in your letter. You said you had all sorts of engagements with the girls and forgot to add boy. You keep me pretty well posted on most things dear, but I guess there are some you do not remember. Yes dear, you are really a good sort of child.

We have had big trouble at our house and Alice is going home soon. Mrs. K found a letter from Joe to Al and I guess it was pretty sweet so she gave Alice the devil. They were both mad as it showed to Mrs. K that Alice had been running around with Joe on the QT. So this made Mrs. K very mad. Sunday there was more trouble for Alice. She and Elsie went walking with two young men who work down in the mill. One of them should have worked Sunday, the one that went with Alice. So when he went to work Monday he got his time for not working Sunday. Alice does not seem to have much success with her fellows as they seem to always get into trouble.

I took Lillie to the dance last night. We, that is Joe, M, Henry and I went up to mothers after the dance. We took a lot of grub we had stolen and had a big feast. I was in agony; we left at 3 o'clock. Lillie had one of her arms around my neck but don't mind dear it is all in the family.

I really don't think you should have broken the Snells agreement. There is no doubt but you are a flirt now dear you don't always give in to me. Now dear when I wrote the letter about the flirt your family did not know that you were going to stay till after the fleet came. For when I was down Friday your mother had just received a letter from you asking to stay so dear I guess you fibbed to me. I should judge by the tone of your letter that you do as you please. I also judged that you figure that the people down there are the only people who want to see you. As you say, they want me to stay, so I am going to stay. But you do not say things want me to come so I will come. Will write more tomorrow as mail is here.

Speaking of engagements you said dear that you could have all sorts of engagements with boys. Well maybe dear you think I could not have all sorts of engagements with girls. Myrtle J. wanted me to come up and see her but I did not go see what I missed. There are numerous other girls that I could make dates with if I wanted to but I won't for there is only one girl and that is enough to keep me good.

I know that you love me dear and want to see me, but even that may not keep you from flirting. Rosa Cadra is stuck on Hack Duffie. He was sitting on her lap at the dance, night before last. She will be as bad as Myrtle Jones the first thing she knows. She was with Myrtle.

I know that Homer would marry Mrs. Shipman as quick as Myrtle. Willie Murphy and I are good friends and he would allow me to take Myrtle if I wanted to.

Dear I miss you a lot. And when I am down to your house I feel as if I would like to put my arms around Lillie as she looks so much like you dear. I love you dear with all your faults more than anything.

The buoy out in the bay has broken loose and is drifting along the coast. Charlie had a close call last night. Do you know that Spaniard they call Shorty, the one that used to follow Lillie. He came at Charlie while he was in Wolf's with a knife about ten inches long, and Charlie grabbed a baseball bat and hit him over the head before he could stick him with the knife. He knocked him senseless.

I think Lillie looked more like you than I ever saw her look and I would not have objected to her putting her arms around me for I could have nearly imagined it was yours.

In your letter dear you spoke of the bar, and wanted to know if I would do that much for you. I should judged dear that you meant drink that much beer for you. Why certainly dear, I would do that much and even more. In fact dear, I would drink a whole keg for you.

I really think you fibbed to me about the flirt, as I was down to your mother's when they were discussing your homecoming and about your staying till the flirt came. Do you always just tell people what you are going to do without considering their wishes in the matter principally when they are concerned. I know you want to see me dear, but I know you want to stay down, and that want is the strongest.

I really did not mean dear about living with K. but just wanted to see what you would say. There are a great many places dear that I would rather live than Crescent City but you can't always live where you would like to.

With Love,
Marius

CHAPTER 14

TRY, TRY AGAIN

The romance between Marius and Helena progressed in the previous chapter, but there was to be no wedding in the year 1908. Perhaps it was the work of the gods. More likely it was the work of the parents. In June the potential bride and groom were still corresponding between the San Francisco bay area and Crescent City. However, their locations had been reversed. Marius was in Berkeley, and Helena was back home in Crescent City. The first letter from the new location seemed to show no change in the relationship:

Berkeley, June 22, 1908

My dearest girl,

I would have written yesterday dear, but did not have time as we played tennis all day long, and I was too tired to write last night. I started a letter to you the other day and just got "my dearest girl" written when I had to go downstairs to do a job for mother. I forgot all about starting the letter. And the next day came upstairs and imagine my surprise on opening my sister's desk to find My Dearest Helena staring me in the face. It is lucky that my sister did not open her desk.

I saw Ed Dozier when I was going to the city the other day, that is Saturday. He got on the car near me. He had a girl and a suitcase. The girl was not bad to look at and was stouter than you are. I spoke to Ed and shook hands with him but he did not ask about you. I then went to the Orpheum that afternoon and sat just a few seats from them. Ed seemed very attentive, so I guess you had better cross him off your list. I forgot to enclose the clipping in that letter so will enclose in this one. Could not find all so will just enclose this one. The bill at Orpheum in city was fair. Saw Bill A standing outside the door and shook hands with him. I don't think he came inside.

The last three nights Hazel Allen has called Miller up and he has been out every time, so when Homer answered the phone last night and Miller was out, he said when he came back into the room, I know that that girl thinks I lied to her and that Miller is here and that I don't want to have her talk to him. Give regards to all the family. With lots of love for my dear girl, Marius

Berkeley, CA
June 24, 1908

My Dear Girl,
    As I have a little time I will drop you a line. Saw Ed Dozier yesterday and had quite a talk with him. Went to Orpheum yesterday with Dorothy. She is not as good looking as she was. She says she is coming up in August. She told me a few things about you also so I had a very interesting day yesterday taking both Dorothy and Ed's information.

    I was going to buy you a bulldog, but the only one I could get is too fierce. He has bit a couple of people so I guess you had better have a more middle tempered dog.

    There is not very much pretty new music dear. In fact there is only one piece I have heard that I like. I think a lot of the leading stars in Oakland are going home. There is no trade. My brother Miller is getting thin. Miller took Hazel Allen to the Orphum Tuesday night. Wednesday when I was there with Dorothy I saw her. She rubbered a good deal, and as she passed me she took a long look.

    I am going over to see mom this afternoon. Bob had a bath yesterday. He is as white as snow. The school Dorothy told me gives a dance tonight, the one you tried to have before you went away.

    Dorothy says that you did not want to come back at all but felt as you ought to. Company has come, so I must close.
With lots of love for my dearest girl,
Yours, Marius

    Now it's back to school for Helena and back to the lumber business for Marius.

    A year has passed. Marius tries again.

Crescent City,

?.8.1909

My dearest Girl Helena,

    It is now nine days since I had a letter from you dear. At first dear I felt pretty sore about it, but now I am really glad for it showed me how much I cared for you dear. When a letter did not come I felt very badly about it and also felt mean all day. In fact showed it so much that people would ask me what was the matter.

    Dear I never asked you to do any thing before, but dear I ask you to come home the next boat as I would like so much to see you dear before I go away. George told Mrs. K tonight that she could go to Oregon when we went. So I guess he means to take me down with him.

    If I don't see you dear before I go to Eureka it might be months before I see you again. As on your coming home next boat really depends whether I will go north or not. I had a dream last night dear that we were furnishing our house, and you were having me select everything, and I thought my how my dear girl has changed.

    This morning, Joe and a bunch of us are going fishing. I was down to see mother in-law last night dear. Be sure to see about your boat early as there will be a crowd coming up. If she does not come back, come on Monday. With lots of love for my dearest only girl, I am yours,
Marius

    The plea to come home must have done it. There were no more letters the rest of the year. The couple finally made it to the altar December 19, 1909. Interesting coverage was provided three days earlier by the local Crescent City paper:

HELENA CRUSIUS AND MARIUS HOTCHKISS TO BE WEDDED IN BERKELEY SUNDAY

    Blushing Maid and Groom-To-Be Sailed on Del Norte Wednesday

    Wedding will Take Place at the Hotchkiss Home

    Young Couple will Return to Reside in Crescent City, Where They Enjoy an Enviable Popularity

Among the passengers on the last Del Norte was a very prominent young couple who were the participants of much good natured jostling and some rice. Many "best wishes" were forced upon them and as each additional congratulation came an added blush was seen to mount to the young woman's face and the half-shy smile of the young man became shyer. The younger crowd gave their well wishes in the hearty manner of youth. The matrons with a reminiscent air of by-gone years, while the old maids bore a pitiably envious expression with here and there a look of sad remorse which seemed to say, "it might have been."

Needless to say that the twain was Miss Helena Crusius and Marius Hotchkiss, whose blushes and shy smiles have become both distinctive and well known during the past year.

Miss Crusius and Mr. Hotchkiss well be married in Berkeley on Sunday, the 19th, at the home of Mr. Hotchkiss' parents.

Miss Helena Crusius was raised in Crescent City, and with the exception of a time spent in school, has lived here all her life. She is one of the best known young women in Del Norte Co. and all of the old residents think of her more as the little child of a few years ago than as of the young woman of today.

Mr. Hotchkiss is the son of W.J. Hotchkiss of San Francisco and Berkeley, president of Hobbs, Wall & Co., and after he had completed his education at Berkeley, came to Crescent City about two years ago, where he has since been employed by the company of which his father is president.

They were originally to have been married in Crescent City and many prominent San Francisco guests were to have been here for the occasion, but owing to the recent storm, which made a landing here very uncertain, it was decided to have the ceremony in Berkeley. Mrs. Frank Crusius, the mother of the "bride-to-be," Mrs. Geo. Keller and Mr. Homer Hotchkiss accompanied the couple on their trip.

We understand that as Mr. and Mrs. Hotchkiss they will return to Crescent City about the 15th of January and make their home here, for a time at least, with Mrs. Crusius.

All the fortunate ones, who have been permitted a squint of the wedding presents, have been astonished at their elegance and richness. Already hundreds of dollars worth of silverware and art works have been received here, and doubtless many more await them in San Francisco.

One of the most beautiful sets of silverware ever seen in this county came from the brother and sister of the late Frank Crusius. As a work of art and beauty, it is simply incomparable.

When the soon-to-be Mr. and Mrs. Hotchkiss return to Crescent City we predict a general old time chiravari, such as is the penalty of popularity and the delight of friends.

A later article described the wedding:

Last Sunday's San Francisco Call contained the following concerning the wedding of Miss Helena Crusius and Mr. M. Hotchkiss:

BERKELEY, Dec. 18 – The wedding of Miss Helena Crusius and Marius Hotchkiss was celebrated this evening at the Hotchkiss home in Claremont, Rev. George Eldridge officiating. Because of the recent death of the father of the bride the ceremony was a simple one and was witnessed only by the immediate relatives and few intimate friends of the bridal couple.

Miss Hazel Hotchkiss attended the bride, while the bridegroom was supported by Henry Snell. Miss Mary Grove acted as ring bearer and Miss Cordelia Grove was flower girl.

The bride was attired in a gown of white satin trimmed with real lace. The maid of honor wore a dress of pink satin trimmed with gold lace. While the marriage service was being read the couple stood beneath a bell of white chrysanthemums. The wedding march was played by Miss Margarette Welsh.

Mrs. Hotchkiss is a daughter of the late F. Crusius and Mrs. Crusius of Crescent City. The bridegroom is a son of Mr. and Mrs. W.J. Hotchkiss of Claremont. He is engaged in the lumber business with his father.

Some things are never forgotten. Edna was the most opinionated of Helena's sisters. Seventy-four years after the wedding, she responded to my request for some of the historical data. At the end of her reply she wrote gratuitously, "I don't know who took over the wedding being in Berkeley, but I do know my mother felt very sad about it as she wanted it to be in Crescent City, where I think it should have been."

Emma had no response, since she had been dead for forty-seven years when Edna wrote.

Edna told me that Marius was one of the nicest people she had ever met. She said it was such a contrast between Marius and Helena, because Helena was mean and could not be trusted.

After the wedding the newlyweds returned to Crescent City. The next few years were not particularly happy. The most important event in their lives was the birth of their only child, Miller Francis Hotchkiss, November 27, 1910. Helena seemed to lack maternal instinct. She was basically cool toward her own son. Marius discovered that Helena fit in very well as somebody who he could make scream at him. There were several times over the years when Helena and Marius lived apart. They always came back together and were living together when Helena died, fifty-nine years after the marriage.

In later years, Miller said that the only thing that really saved him was the intervention of Helena's sisters, who did their full share of raising him. Sadly, there were far too many times Miller was present when Helena and Marius were fighting. Miller said one of them would turn toward him suddenly and say, "What do you think, Sonny?"

Lillian's daughter, Fran, spoke of Helena's coldness. The family did not notice it as much when Helena was growing up. It seemed to appear after Helena married Marius. Helena also began to lord it over her sisters, who became somewhat afraid of her.

Helena did her full share of yelling back at Marius, but she was also capable of the soft barbed comment. Years later Marius and Helena visited Lillian and family for dinner. Helena waited for quite a while after dinner had been served and then said, "You will notice that one of the men at this table has not unfolded his napkin."

The comment did not surprise Lillian. She had already given

advance warning to her family, "You will be happy to see your Aunt Helena and Uncle Marius. If they are a little different, well that's alright."

Marius knew what Helena's name was when he wrote letters to her, but after the marriage he started calling her Helen. I believe it was just one more little thing that Marius had dreamed up to irritate Helena, not calling her by her correct name. Nobody ever challenged Marius about the name, so she was "Helen" to him and Helena to everybody else for the rest of her life.

Fran said that there was one time that she remembers in Crescent City that a dinner guest actually said, "Marius, why do you call her Helen? Everybody knows that her name is Helena."

Marius had no answer for this, so he gave none. There was total dead silence at the table until somebody mercifully changed the subject.

CHAPTER 15

THE CRUSIUS FAMILY

The Crusius family is from Kaiserslautern, Germany. The family was quite successful and even known as, "Kaiserslautern's Famous Family". In addition to being a "Metzgermeister" or a master butcher, Franz Crusius and his wife Regina, also owned two large bookstores. The butcher shop occupied the entire ground floor of a four story building. The extended family lived in the upper floors.

Franz's son, Ludwig, emigrated to America. Uncle Louie, as he was called, was initially responsible for bringing the Crusius blood to Crescent City, California. Though he married in Germany he and his soon to be ex wife moved to California, where he, like his father, owned and operated a butcher shop. Louie and his wife divorced in 1878, and had no children of their own.

Uncle Louie's older brother Heinrich lived and died in Germany, but his oldest son, Franz (Frank) Crusius, found his way to San Francisco and later joined Uncle Louie in Crescent City. Frank came in 1871 during a time when families who could afford to, sent their sons away in hope of protecting them from the Franco-Prussian War. Frank's first wife, Caroline, passed away at the age of thirty-one. Fifteen months after Caroline's death Frank met his future wife, Barbara Moock, in San Francisco.

Barbara was also a German immigrant, and was working as a housekeeper for a family whom Frank often visited. Frank courted Barbara for two weeks and they were soon married in San Francisco at St. Mark's Lutheran Church.

The newlyweds moved to Crescent City where Frank went to work for Uncle Louie in his butcher shop. Subsequently, Frank went into administrative politics. He served as the county treasurer until his death. He did not live to see Helena married, dying in San Francisco three months before the wedding.

Helena, the oldest daughter, was born December 7, 1889 in Crescent City. It has been said that Frank and Barbara wanted one of their daughters to marry a Hotchkiss. In the fall of 1907 Helena was almost eighteen. The next oldest daughter was only sixteen. Marius ended up as the chosen husband, since he was living in Crescent City at the time. The Hotchkiss' business was a major force in the local economy, well connected and powerful.

The desire to have a daughter marry a Hotchkiss spread through the community. Four years later Edna McVay, the daughter of County Auditor N. G. McVay, married Homer Hotchkiss, Marius' brother. It did not end there because Marius' son Miller also married a girl from Crescent City.

Lillian (Lill) was the oldest of Helena's four sisters. She is mentioned frequently in Marius' letters to Helena. Following in her sister's footsteps, Lill attended the Snell Academy in Berkeley. At the time of her father's death, her mother, Barbara, had sunk into a depression so deep that it ultimately ended Lill's school days. Barbara was forty-two when her husband died. She died eight years later.

Lillian married Chester Royal Ward in 1920, and soon had three children of her own. More than one written family remembrance speaks of Aunt Lillian being happily busy in the kitchen. The warmest of Miller's aunts, Lill found a full life in the kitchen in Crescent City.

Sisters Fran and Gertrude had little influence on Helena's little family. Fran married a German citizen and moved to Germany. Gertrude, the youngest, was only nine years old when Helena married.

Edna was thirteen years old when Marius and Helena tied the knot.
She became a school teacher and rode the Hobbs Wall train to her first teaching job in nearby Fort Dick. Later, she moved to Knightsen, California and lived with Helena and Marius for a year. She was Miller's first school teacher.

Edna later married Colonel William Robert McMaster. After marriage she often went overseas on assignments with her husband and lived a life of luxury with all kinds of servants. Edna, similar to her sister, was not known as a warm mother and often neglected her children. However, Edna thought that Helena was a terrible person, and in contrast thought the very best of Marius.

The warmth that Edna displayed to Miller whenever she was

home from overseas was probably her way of demeaning Helena.

Edna's son, William H. McMaster (Bill), was a West Point graduate, who left his military career to become a nuclear physicist. The army had sent him to the University of Virginia for two years of post graduate study of nuclear physics. At the end of the two year period, the army planned to transfer him to a remote post with no connection with what he had been studying.

Bill tried to explain that his field was growing so rapidly that two years away would create a knowledge gap that he could never recover from. Their educational investment in him would have been wasted.

The army didn't seem to care, so Bill resigned his commission and continued his studies. After receiving his PhD he went on to work at Lawrence Laboratory in Livermore, California, where he ended his career. He led a research team in Alaska during the International Geophysical Year. While in Alaska he befriended Reverend Gene Rebert, who taught him the art of woodcarving. After Bill retired he taught woodcarving and also created carvings of his own.

In Germany Uncle Louie's sisters made good marriages and established successful but tragic descendants. Magdalena and Johanna Crusius married brothers, Franz Pfaff and George Michael Pfaff. The Pfaff family was another well known, wealthy family in Kaiserslautern, Germany. The Pfaff's were known for their proficient craftsmanship abilities. Franz, Magdalena's husband was a skilled instrument worker and his brother George Michael, Johanna's husband, was the founder of the Pfaff Sewing Machine Company which is still prominent today.

However, success and international fame did not necessarily bring happiness to this family. Johanna's first two children died at the ages of 17 and 13. She had three more children with distinguished but tragic lives. George Michael Jr. and Lina, never married. They ran the company from 1893 to 1926, George for 24 years until his death, then Lina for 9 more years until her retirement at the age of 72. Lina was a distinguished and honored citizen, and in 1926 was the only woman in Germany to receive the title "Kommerzienratin" that was awarded to distinguished businesspersons.

Jakob, the fifth child was in sales and advertising and did fairly well for himself. However the tragedy occurred when Jakob committed suicide at the age of 33.

Jakob's son Karl, Johanna's only grandchild, assumed management after Lina retired and was responsible for the international expansion of the company during his 26-year tenure. Unfortunately like his father, he also was a suicide.

The net family result for Johanna was 4 children who never married, two of them dying before maturity. Her fifth child was a suicide, as was her only grandchild. Her husband, the founder of the company, also lived long enough to see the suicide of Jakob.

CHAPTER 16

KNIGHTSEN RANCH

The town of Knightsen was founded by George Knight in 1898. The Santa Fe Railway had just completed its survey for a route through Eastern Contra Costa County, serving the delta of the Sacramento and San Joaquin rivers. This was the richest farmland in the State of California. Santa Fe built a station. Knight got himself appointed postmaster and built a general store. The trains started rolling through in 1900.

This was all happening less than fifty miles from Berkeley. Was it all interesting to W.J. Hotchkiss? Certainly! In 1918 the *Byron Times* looked back over the preceding sixteen years:

W.J. HOTCHKISS, DELTA LAND OWNER

"For the past sixteen years W.J. Hotchkiss has been prominently identified with the great Delta sections of Central California, owning extensive holdings in San Joaquin and Contra Costa counties, located in the richest and most productive territory, where peat and sediment soils produce abundant harvests under systematic operating methods.

"The first venture in this interesting Delta country was made by Mr. Hotchkiss in 1904, when he purchased an interest in what is now the Sand Mound property, a tract of some 2300 acres located in the Knightsen section, where modern irrigation methods and practical farming experience produce splendid crops each season. He also owns 3100 acres on the Bethel Tract."

There were risks in farming the Delta. The big levee break on Jersey Island before 1910 wiped out much of the Knightsen land that was under cultivation. W.J. fought back with the aid of the Reclamation District, building bigger and stronger levees. The farming methods on Hotchkiss properties were state of the art. The *Byron Times* continues:

"On these holdings wonderful results are obtained in the growing of alfalfa, handling of extensive dairy interests, and shipment of almost a thousand gallons of milk daily from Knightsen to Oakland creameries. One feature of the district is the magnificent herd of Holstein dairy cows.

"Special tracts are devoted to staple products of the Delta, such crops as potatoes, beans, onions, asparagus, celery, etc. a tract of 235 acres devoted to asparagus produced a wonderful showing this season, while 400 acres in potatoes added new records to the Hotchkiss achievements. Sugar beets have also grown here to wonderful perfection.

"The splendid system of improvements and developments show the care and attention, as well as energetic ability of the Hotchkiss methods, demonstrating that this landowner keeps pace with conditions while being ever on the alert to do things that count for greater results.
"This Hotchkiss way of farming means much to the Delta......"

George Knight must have visualized Knightsen, with its convenient railroad station, as the center of a substantial dairy industry. It didn't take long for W.J. to figure this out. In 1918 Knightsen was shipping over 2,500 gallons of milk per day from six dairies to Oakland and other Bay Area cities. Almost forty percent of the total came from W.J. Most of his production went to Standard Creameries, which he owned. That company specialized in ice cream, distributing to the East Bay, Sacramento and Bakersfield. The company used the technical expertise of Professor G. D. Turnbow of the University of California at Davis.

W.J. made several improvements to his property, including building a large canal for irrigation. The canal is still in use today. The only move that he made that might have been subject to question by some is the appointment of Marius Hotchkiss as manager. It is not clear when Marius left Crescent City and moved to Knightsen. The first confirmed date in Knightsen is 1920. He was still there in 1923, probably leaving in 1925 or 1926 for the ranch in Mexico.

Reclamation District 799 included 2,000 acres of Hotchkiss land. W.J. was the President and head of the Board of Directors, reasonable since he owned two thirds of the land. This was one of many small districts which were formed to reclaim and protect the Delta land. The district had only one paid employee, whose only job was to keep the pump running so that the farmland would not be flooded. Marius had this job, and he was paid twenty-five dollars per month for it. There is no known record of pump failure during Marius' time. He was either very skilled or very lucky.

Marius was nominally in charge of the dairy operations. In truth, there had to be a strong second in command. Dairy management is basically a 24/7 job with only brief time off. Marius spent the weekends at Berkeley. Gaga would not stand for it if one of her children was less than fifty miles away and did not come home for the weekend. There had to be another cow person taking over at the ranch.

Miller Hotchkiss was born in 1910, so he attended the Iron House School in Knightsen, a currently revered one room elementary schoolhouse. Helena's sister, Edna, was the schoolteacher in Miller's first year. Undoubtedly, the whole thing was orchestrated by W.J. to make the transition easier for Helena. In practice, Edna got to hear both Helena and Marius yelling at each other. It was the only time that Edna had lived with the feuding couple. She had to choose between the two sides. For the rest of her life she proclaimed that Marius was almost perfect, and Helena was a bum.

W. J. provided a beautiful house on the property for the family to live in. The land and the house were acquired by the Dal Porto family in the 1930's after Bank of America foreclosed on W.J. The property has recently been subdivided. There is no record that Marius did anything bad while at Knightsen. He probably didn't do much good either.

There is one letter from this period that Helena saved. Marius wrote to her while she was away in Crescent City. The envelope was dated August 17, 1923. Note that Marius had already descended to calling Helena by the name Helen in writing. Helena did not like this, but she must have gotten used to it eventually.

Dear Helen,
 I will write you a few lines today as I must send the check that came for you as I do not like to have so much money around the house loose. I am going out now to get a milker, hope he is a good one. I received your letters mailed Monday this morning. You must tell me when you figure on leaving as I can stop writing as I do not want any letters to get there after you leave. I am sorry that every body thinks you have such a hard time and have to go in rags. But I suppose it can not be helped. I had a talk with Anderson this morning and he said the Pons are always overdrawn, that they seem to figure that as long as there is blank check in the book they can draw check. I am going to town to get a milker. I hope he stays. The Nixons are coming over tonight, the Pons gave the invitation. You raised hell when you started to get things changed there. Your friend L. came home yesterday with a dozen

bananas. I got the tag. They were charged to us, but they disappeared. I have not seen hair nor hide of them. The bunch from Victor's was in Knightsen last night. Ethel has not been out to see me. She certainly must know that you are in C. C. yet, and the coast is clear. With lots of love for you, dear.
    Yours,
    Marius

P.S. Hope son catches a lot of fish.

Another relative, Will Grove, came on the scene in 1912. He was Emma's oldest brother. If Emma's relatives had any money, W.J. felt it was his job to see that they invested with him. In this case the two men partnered and bought another 917 acres out of the total of 2,937 that were in the reclamation district.

Will and Emma's other brothers had all worked for their uncle, John Rankin Hite, a wealthy gold miner. Will had played a major role in the relationship between his sister and her husband. It was he who, acting on the orders of Uncle John, bought the ranch in Healdsburg that was close to the Hotchkiss ranch. Emma and her parents settled on the ranch. She was eventually courted as "the girl next door".

In the late nineteenth century one of the best routes to Yosemite was by stagecoach to the Hite mine on the South Fork of the Merced River. At that point the travelers went on by horseback to Yosemite. Uncle Gus Hite had built the needed hotel on the site, and he ran it until his untimely early death. Will then took over the management of the hotel. He was a good man and a good manager. He definitely must have been looking over Marius' shoulder at Knightsen for the benefit of the family.

Will was born in 1846. He was well over ninety when he died. Sometime in the 1930's he moved to the Hotchkiss ranch in Yountville, where he spent his last days. There are two remaining events in his life that deserve to be mentioned. He made the newspapers when he took his first airplane ride at the age of ninety-seven.

The other event came soon after Miller Hotchkiss had graduated from the University of California in 1932. It may have been the first chore that W.J. asked of Miller. The word had trickled down that when

Will was collecting the monthly rent from the tenants, he would pinch the ladies. Miller said later that he had no trouble with the assignment. He told Will to just stop it, and if he didn't, Miller was going to send Emma to talk to him.

CHAPTER 17

MEXICAN LAND CLAIM

It was a simple little deal. The Mexican government was seeking foreign investment. W.J. was always looking for an opportunity to make money. In the year 1925 he bought land for fifty thousand dollars and pumped in roughly another thirty thousand for equipment, buildings and start up expenses. All he had to do was sit back and wait for the profits to come in. There were no profits. A portion of the invested capital was finally recovered through the American Mexican Claims Commission which was established by the U. S. government.

Nayarit is a state on the western coast of Mexico. Its capitol is Tepic. This was an area with a fine coastal area with excellent climate, abundant rains in the summer and very fertile soils. A battery of Mexican attorneys determined that W.J. could acquire clear title to twenty thousand acres for fifty thousand dollars. The land was fertile but totally unimproved with unbroken soil and an abundant crop of weeds.

It turned out that W.J. was not alone in the venture. It was for sure he didn't have much time to devote to the project, but Mr. C.A. Vance did. He also had twelve thousand five hundred dollars in cash to contribute to the purchase. He went to Mexico to manage the project.

W.J. was known in California for his advanced modern farming practices. These were applied in Mexico. There were two major problems that arose. First, if Vance could get a crop raised, the nomadic Indian population would come down from the hills in the night and harvest the crop for themselves.

The second problem was much more serious. A group of a hundred and fifty armed men came from time to time and took over the land that had been developed. They claimed ownership of the land, backed by a nebulous early agrarian reform act and with an absolute minimum of paperwork. The bottom line was that the state authorities backed them up. Attempts at negotiation failed, and Vance came home when there was no more land to farm. The agrarian reformers received developed farmland for free, and they even got to observe the modern farming practices. One of the sympathetic Mexican authorities remarked that the Americans had given them more than the benefit of establishing an agricultural college.

The good news was that the United States government established a commission to claim reimbursement for its citizens. The bad news was that the United States government established a commission. At their best, these outfits take a long time to get anything done. They are also bureaucratic in their ways and difficult to work with. The final settlement payment did not come until the year 1956. The net payout after considerable legal expense was about thirty percent of the original investment.

The claim by Vance was handled separately. It was finally determined that the Hotchkiss group invested thirty-nine thousand dollars. If you have read this far in the book, you are surely aware that W.J. always tried to invest as little as possible of his own money in any venture. He did very well in selling participation in this particular venture. In fact, his total investment was zero. Who was the big investor? Marius W. Hotchkiss, of course, his contribution was twenty-seven thousand!

It is hard to believe that Marius in 1925 had accumulated that kind of money. He probably didn't. W.J. was quite adept at shuffling land ownership and enterprise participation among his children and his various interests. It would have been easy for him to create wealth for Marius. It would have been worth it for W.J., because Marius did spend a lot of time in Mexico, far away from anything in California that he could foul up for his father. This was one more venture where Marius had a title but no real responsibility. It is especially interesting that a thorough search of a stack of papers half a foot high reveals no mention of Marius in Mexico, but he was definitely there. He talked about it, often at length, and even Marius could have figured out that it would be a good idea to keep watch over an investment where he owned over half.

CHAPTER 18

BRIDGING THE GOLDEN GATE

On January 13, 1923, a group of a hundred prominent men met in Santa Rosa in support of a bridge across the Golden Gate. The gathering was the culmination of a lot of talk and calls for action. Finally, this was the action. James Rolph, The Mayor of San Francisco, spoke as did other prominent people from San Francisco and the northern counties. Action was specific and important. They formed the Bridging the Golden Gate Association.

The executive committee was carefully chosen to advance the purpose of the Association. These powerful and enthusiastic men were to rally support from the public for a bridge. Second, they were to draft legislation authorizing the establishment of the Golden Gate Bridge and Highway District.

Frank Doyle was a prominent banker in Santa Rosa and head of the local Chamber of Commerce. The organizational meeting had been held in the Chamber's meeting room. His membership on the executive committee provided a solid foundation.

Richard J. Welch was an up and coming member of the San Francisco Board of Supervisors. His influence was important locally and also later when he was elected to the United States House of Representatives. Another member enthusiast from San Francisco was Captain I. J. Hibbard.

Frank L. Coombs was an Assemblyman from Napa. He introduced the legislation to establish the bridge district. This was to be the first time ever, that local property owners joined in a local tax district for the purpose of building a bridge. The legislation was passed May 25, 1923.

The executive committee chose Joseph B. Strauss as its engineer. Strauss had already spent two years promoting the bridge actively. He was to stay with the project to its very successful ending.

After the January meeting, three men embarked on journeys to California's northern counties, speaking to anyone who would listen to them, encouraging all to support the bridge. These three important people were Joseph B. Strauss, consulting engineer, Thomas Allen Box, long time supporter of the bridge, and the sixty-five year old W.J. Hotchkiss, Chairman of the Executive Committee of the Bridging the Golden Gate Association. It would be fourteen long years before the dream of these great men was realized.

Guidebooks will tell you that this was to be at that time the world's longest and tallest single span suspension bridge. Each of the massive cables was over thirty-six inches in diameter and weighed eleven thousand tons. They will also say quite correctly that this is one of the most beautiful objects that mankind has ever created. People from the world over come to the San Francisco bay area to admire the bridge across the Golden Gate. Guidebooks will not tell you that it was easier to build it than it was to get the darned thing approved.

In San Francisco Focus magazine of May, 1987, Tom Horton wrote, "To clear a way so the bridge could be built, proponents had to contend with professional and amateur doubters and doomsayers, scheming politicians, crooked lobbyists, the War Department, dissenting engineers, earthquake alarms, early environmentalists, legislative roadblocks, court tests, taxpayer revolts, insidious whispering campaigns, scurrilous rumors, a depression economy, a Southern Pacific conspiracy, a horrible bridge design and a chief bridge engineer without the right bridge building credentials."

It could not have been an accident that W.J. was named as the head of the executive committee. In fact, the whole deal looks like something that W.J. would have created. Each member of the committee had his purpose. He was there for a reason. The great visionary, the dreamer who had the ability to choose men who would carry out his dreams had found another project. The bridge was to be his greatest achievement.

Strauss understood. In his 1937 report to the Board of Directors of the Golden Gate Bridge and Highway District Strauss wrote:

"The services that Mr. Hotchkiss rendered the Association were invaluable. He gave it not only his own time but the necessary financial support, and, together with the writer, carried the principal burden during the long and trying preorganization period."

Strauss and W.J. were two of a kind, promoter-developers. Their greatest success came from their leadership and their choice of assistants. The literature is filled with challenges to Strauss as the bridge designer. Credit is sought for one or more of the engineers that Strauss employed. The most credible candidate is Charles Ellis. W.J. would have answered all of these questions the same way. He would say, "Strauss gave Ellis the opportunity to do a wonderful job. Both men deserve full credit. Neither could have succeeded without the other. The project was to get the bridge built."

Both Strauss and W.J. were goal driven. Their common goal was to build a bridge. Although Strauss had a much stronger ego, he always supported W.J. for the common good. W.J. recognized Strauss' importance for the project and never got in his way.

In the year 1994 the San Francisco Examiner launched an editorial in support of Ellis' claim to fame as the bridge designer. At the same time they spoke eloquently about the contributions of San Francisco city engineer Michael O'Shaughnessy. Personally, I wish Ellis, O'Shaughnessy and the Examiner well. However, I was inclined to take pen in hand in support of my favorite cause. On March 7, 1994, I wrote to the editor:

"I read with great interest your Sunday editorial on stealing the Golden Gate Bridge. I know little about the exploits of Strauss, Ellis and O'Shaughnessy, but I am not surprised that history often needs to have the books rebalanced.

"While you are at it, how about extra credit to my grandfather, W.J. Hotchkiss, one more person without whom the bridge never would have been built.

"A bridge is made of steel. Its girders and the design they are formed into are there for all to see and wonder at for decades. The hard fought political and economic battles remain behind the scenes. These days perhaps we could call them the software of the bridge.

"From the beginning W.J. Hotchkiss was one of the primary leaders of the fight to overcome the obstacles to the bridge. The enclosed cartoon from your own editorial page of 71 years ago clearly identifies who supported the bridge."

I finished by offering a series of quotations about W.J. from several published books.

CHAPTER 19

POET, BUSINESSMAN, GOD

Strauss had more than incidental ability as a poet, and some of his work has been preserved. W.J. stuck to prose, but his prose soared into the world of glorious poetry when he spoke of the bridge. He spoke on the radio June 21, 1923:

"The Bridge across the Golden Gate, when completed, will be the greatest mechanical accomplishment of its kind yet constructed by the hands of men. It may well be said to be the Eighth wonder of the world. It will be built from plans and specifications taken from a new form of cantilever construction, designed by J.B. Strauss, bridge engineer of Chicago. The main span will be 4,000 feet between piers, and more than double that of any other bridge span in the world. This span will be 210 feet above the water, a height greater than the tallest ship, and under which all the fleets and navies of the world can freely pass. The approaches to these piers from the adjacent shores total 2,640 feet, thus making the total length of the bridge 6,640 feet, or 1.6 miles. The width of the bridge is eighty feet, and provides for two lines of trolley cars, two lines of automobiles in each direction, and two seven foot side walks.

"San Francisco is at present water cramped on three sides. The history of large cities proves that they can only expand by direct connection with adjoining shores. With the Golden Gate Bridge completed, San Francisco will be freed from the cramping natural conditions which have retarded her growth.

"It would be hard to estimate the financial and economic benefits accruing by reason of the building of the Golden Gate Bridge. The greatest benefit will come, of course, first to San Francisco. The next greatest benefit will come to those sections immediately adjacent to the northern terminus of the Bridge, and every part of the state will be benefited by the wonderful growth that will follow that completion of this eighth wonder of the world. The mighty achievements wrought by the children of men in this wonderful time in which we live follow each other in such quick succession that the accomplishment of one great feat is soon followed by another greater still. But it is the firm belief of the speaker that when the Golden Gate Bridge has been completed, and there has been woven into the story of its building, as there must inevitably be, the glamour of the romance of the days of '49, the line of the yellow poppied fields, and the sun kissed landscape of California, the minds of the people of the world will pause longer in contemplation of this wonderful achievement than of any other that has preceded it, and there will come, even from the far ends of the earth, the people of every land to look upon this crowning creation of the brains, and the genius of men whose pillars are the gate posts of the portal thru which, in this and future generations, will pass the fleets of all nations, bearing the riches of the world to pour them into the lap of the people, who, by the grace and will of God, have been given the privilege of living in this favored land.

"The mariners of old who sailed the merchant ships of Tyre thru the straits guarded on each side by the Pillars of Hercules, are said to have read in the rock faces of the sentinels of the sea, the anger and wrath of the God storms. Like these Pillars of Hercules, the pillars of the Bridge stand like guardians of the Golden Gate, but instead of speaking woe and disaster, their towering heights seem to point the way to loftier aims, and greater ambitions for the sons of men."

That was W.J. Hotchkiss, the prose poet, soaring along with his dream. However, the same man was also a hard headed businessman. Have you ever thought about how much money you can make when you own a bridge?

The thought more than crossed W.J.'s mind. He wrote a newspaper article on the subject:

GOLDEN GATE BRIDGE OFFICIAL TELLS OF VALUE OF PUBLICLY OWNED BRIDGE

CARQUINEZ BRIDGE TRAFFIC PROOF OF NEED FOR PUBLIC SUPPORT OF GATE SPAN, DECLARES HOTCHKISS

BY W.J. HOTCHKISS
Chairman of Executive Committee, Bridging the Golden Gate Association

"Travel is crossing the Carquinez Straits on the Carquinez Bridge. The building of this grand structure is the greatest event that has happened to the people on each side of that body of water since the Southern Pacific Railroad crossed these straits many years ago.

"The importance of the completion of this bridge, and the far reaching effect it is going to have on the growth and prosperity of the people it serves, is appreciated or understood at this time only in a small degree. Pages could be written, setting out in detail the manner and degree of these benefits. The text of that story would be taken from Adam Smith's text book on political economy which says: "Prosperity and business increases in proportion to population and contact of people."

"This article is not written to show the great benefit this bridge will be to the people of California, but to point out the mistake the people make in not building such bridges themselves. We will take this bridge for example. There is an old fool law that probably came down to us in that Pandora Box in which was brought to us the English statute on riparian rights. This old law said that the right to bridge a stream was vested in the political authority governing the land on the left bank of said stream. Under this authority, the County of Contra Costa had the authority to build a bridge across the Carquinez Straits. There came along some bridge promoters from the East and they asked the Supervisors of Contra Costa County to give them the privilege of building a bridge across Carquinez Straits. The Supervisors gave them that privilege. I have been told that, for the consideration of the gift, that after twenty-five years the bridge should belong to Contra Costa County. The right to build this bridge was an asset of the people of Contra Costa County, the same as the Court House or any other property that the people of the County owned. Let us see what kind of a trade the people of Contra Costa made when they disposed of this valuable asset.

"The first day the bridge was opened 14,000 automobiles crossed the bridge. The toll on an automobile is 60 cents and 10 cents for each passenger. It is reasonable to suppose that there would be 4 persons in each car, which would make one dollar per car, or $14,000 for that one day. Of course there is not going to be 14,000 automobiles crossing the bridge every day now, but long before the twenty-five year is up, there will be many more than 14,000 automobiles crossing the bridge each day. Anyway, on the second day, 9,000 automobiles crossed. The writer drove over the bridge yesterday, a holiday, and it looked to him that another 14,000 or more automobiles would cross during the day. 14,000 automobiles at $1 each would be about $5,110,000 per year. Other revenue, it is reasonable to suppose would amount to $60,000, or a gross income of say $5,170,000 per year.

"There were four ticket takers at the bridge heads yesterday, say $25 per day, or approximately $10,000 per year. Add $40,000 per year for upkeep and we have say $50,000 per year for operation and upkeep.

"If the bridge had been built by the people of Contra Costa County, bonds could have been sold to build it at 4½ per cent, or an annual interest charge of $270,000. Add $50,000 for upkeep and operation and you have a charge of $320,000 per year. Subtract $320,000 from $5,170,000 which leaves $4,850,000 profit per year. $4,850,000 multiplied by 25 years is exactly $121,250,000. Subtract $6,000,000, the cost of the bridge, from $121,250,000 and there remains a net profit of $115,250,000. A very nice profit on an investment of $6,000,000.

"If the people of Contra Costa county had built the bridge themselves, that is what they would have had, and the bridge also. As it is, the promoters will have the $115,250,000 and the people of Contra Costa County will have only the bridge.

"I do not know how much taxes the people of Contra Costa County pay, but I will venture the assertion that this natural resource which nature bestowed on them would have freed them from the burden of taxes forever.

"I have been told that the people of Minnesota pay all of their taxes from royalties on iron ore which some wise statesman managed to save for the people.

"Some one may say that the Carquinez Bridge cost $8,000,000 instead of $6,000,000, and that the money to build it cost more than 4½ %. Even so if true there would be but little taken off the $115,250,000. Also it may be said that the Railroad Commission will regulate the tolls so that no such profits, as stated, will be allowed to be made. That may be true also, but if the bridge had been built by the people of Contra Costa County, organized as a Bridge and Highway District, the Railroad Commission would have no authority to regulate the tolls.

"On the eve of the organization of the Golden Gate Bridge and

Highway District, and in answer to the opposition of certain interests to this great public enterprise, this article is written so that the people of San Francisco and the North Bay Counties who will compose the District, can better understand the great opportunity a wise providence has placed in their hands for the betterment of the people of the State of California, and more particularly of the people of the Golden Gate Bridge and Highway District."

W.J. never had to face the problems of today. I wonder what stand he would have taken on pouring bridge tolls into money losing bus and ferry service. Would we have seen W.J., the dreamer or W.J., the hard headed businessman? You can only be sure that W.J. would have studied the issue carefully before making his decision. If he wrote on the subject, you can be sure he would have written eloquently. The above article by W.J. is included here in its entirety so that you can see how well he structured his material.

It would have been helpful if God had taken a hand in enabling the bridge. However, Herbert W. Slater of the Santa Rosa Press Democrat figured that God's help was probably not needed. W.J. Hotchkiss was involved in the project, and he would take care of everything.

W.J Hotchkiss Eminently Qualified to Engineer Building of Bay Bridge
Press Democrat- Santa Rosa California July 28, 1923

By. Herbert W. Slater

"Renewed impetus in the bridging of the Golden Gate has followed the meeting held last Wednesday in Napa, at which J.B Strauss, the eminent engineer, who designed the coming 'Eighth Wonder of the World,' again explained the plans, and pointed out the feasibility of the construction.

"Some weeks since I mentioned in these columns that Sonoma County is naturally proud that an old Sonoma County boy, W.J. Hotchkiss, or as most of us know him in friendliness as 'Joe Hotchkiss,' is taking such a prominent part in bringing the bridging of the Golden Gate to pass. Mention was also made at the time, of the great part Mr. Hotchkiss had taken in the development and success of great enterprises involving millions of dollars, just as the big bridge across the bay will take millions to build.

Chapter Raised Near Healdsburg

"While Mr. Hotchkiss still owns the old Hotchkiss ranch on the Russian River and has other property interests in the county, there are undoubtedly many new people here who need some sort of an introduction to him, so that they too may realize why he is mentioned as a leader in finance and business, widely know all over the Pacific Coast and in the East, and heralded as a great factor in the bridging of the Golden Gate.

"Here are a few glimpses into Mr. Hotchkiss's life since boyhood, indicating that he has been a man of deeds and one who has just claim to mention and a place in the foremost ranks of those who have been most successful:

"As a boy Mr. Hotchkiss lived on a farm near Healdsburg. His early life taught him the needs of the farm and acquainted him with a broad field of agricultural development. He acted as manager, and in fact organized the first cooperative farmers' marketing organization in California.

Chapter Built Canneries

"He built canneries in many counties of the state. He was organizer and then president of the Central California Canneries, the second largest fruit canning concern in California. He was one of the organizers and is vice president of the California Packing Corporation. It is a fact, too, that Joe Hotchkiss is one of the largest farmers in California. At the present time he owns and has in a high state of production big farms in Napa, Sonoma, San Joaquin, Contra Costa and Stanislaus counties. His farms are producing prunes, apples, asparagus, potatoes, beans and corn.

Chapter Has Lumber Interests

"Mr. Hotchkiss is also a big lumberman; he owns redwood mills in Del Norte and Mendocino counties. He is President of Hobbs-Wall & Co., and The Hotchkiss Redwood Company.

"I must not forget to also state that Joe Hotchkiss is one of the largest dairymen in California: he organized and became president of the East Bay Milk Producers Association, a co-operative marketing organization of dairymen, supplying most of the milk to Berkeley, Oakland, and east bay cities. He was for years vice President and largest stockholder in the Port Blakeley Mill Company, which had the largest saw mill in the world.

"Mr. Hotchkiss has a breadth of vision that looks to the future, and centers upon such a project as a bridge across the Golden Gate as being the most important factor in the development of Northern California, and including the north of Bay Counties.

"More than that, he recognizes that the bridging of the bay will benefit the whole of California. He has gone into facts and figures and has studied all details most carefully. In questions of business and finance his judgment is eagerly sought.

"He is a tireless worker and can hardly find enough hours in the day to attend to all the demands upon his time. But he is ever ready to put his shoulder to the wheel just as he is doing now to promote the gigantic span across the bay, when he knows that the task can be accomplished and the goal so worthy of attaining when the future of California is considered.

"So Sonoma County may well be proud that Joe Hotchkiss's name is linked as a leader in the bridging of the Golden Gate. I share the personal pride felt by others in this matter; many of us have known Mr. Hotchkiss these many years, and when we hear him say that the big bridge can be built, and that the financing of the big scheme can be readily assured, we know that he means what he says."

CHAPTER 20

A LONG AND GLORIOUS PATHWAY TO OBSCURITY

It is not the purpose of this book to detail the painful progress toward eventual authorization and construction of the bridge. That story has been told many times by others. The solid organization that was set up in 1923 persevered and prevailed. W.J. was still active in the 1920's, and his name would surface from time to time. He continued his promotion of the bridge, and he spoke out loud and clear when it was appropriate. If he needed to be reminded what "God" was supposed to do, Herbert W. Slater was there to remind him. On May 27, 1923, after the governor had signed the enabling bill, Slater wrote:

"But in the meantime such men as W. 'Joe' Hotchkiss have been untiring at work going over the great project in all its details with Engineer Strauss, men of finance and others, until the great undertaking is ready to move."

The next step was the approval of the War Department. This was rather essential. The land at both ends of the bridge was owned by the federal government as military bases, and the federal government also had power to control what went in between. Federal approval of anything takes a while, but eventually tentative approval was granted December 20, 1924. The announcement was by wire to W.J. Hotchkiss. Although temporary, the authorization definitely committed the government, so that the project could move forward.

It was predictable that the San Francisco Board of Supervisors would not go along with the district formation easily. W.J. was there in 1925 and 1926 to try to help things along. At one particular meeting there was hot debate about what were basically two versions of the same declaration in support of the bridge. One version had been proposed by Richard J. Welch, W.J.'s colleague. W.J. told the supervisors that they were under obligation to pass the Welch ordinance and let the people decide whether they wanted a bridge. Supervisor Hayden objected vehemently, "Don't you think the people look to us for information as to how they should act on the proposition?"

W.J. replied, "If they depend on one supervisor, they wouldn't know anything," He then went on to explain that he was not referring to

Hayden personally.

Eventually the Golden Gate Bridge and Highway District was incorporated December 4, 1928. W.J. Hotchkiss was involved in one more controversy. The San Francisco Board of Supervisors named three of its own members as directors of the new district, and provoked a fire storm of protest. The statement released by W.J. in his official capacity was as follows:

"The executive committee of five men that has, after six years' continuous work, brought to a successful conclusion the formation of the district owe their success largely to the fact that they desired to create and conduct a great public utility free from politics, politicians and political influence, except insofar as was necessary within its own organization.

"The dream of the committee was a public utility, organized by the people, whose government would be intrusted to officials chosen from the mass of the people and not from the body of officials already holding office.

"This is not in any way intended to cast reflection on the character of men in public service but is based on the presumption that the duties of the offices they already hold should take all their time and ability and might interfere with their duties as directors of the Bridge and Highway District.

"This idea of the committee has been followed out in the appointment of directors from all the counties of the district except San Francisco. The Supervisors of San Francisco appointed as directors of the Golden Gate Bridge and Highway District are perhaps as well qualified for the position as any men that could be appointed, but before accepting the appointments they should resign from the office they already hold.

"Before the Golden Gate Bridge can be commenced there will have to be voted bonds by the people to build it. The people are a little "gun shy" on the voting of bonds and if they are not entirely satisfied they will not vote the bonds.

"Powerful opposition was encountered by the committee in the formation of the bridge district, but these interests did not take the matter seriously until it was too late to kill its formation. This opposition will be carried into the building of the bridge and there should be given by its proponents as little ground as possible for defeat."

One of the three supervisors withdrew his name in an act of conscience. The other two routinely participated in the initial meeting of the Board of directors on January 23, 1929. Frank Doyle and Richard Welch were the only men who transferred from the Bridging the Golden Gate Executive Committee to the new Board. The other continuity was in the first action of the Board. They appointed Strauss as Chief Engineer. They also appointed George H. Harlan as attorney. Harlan's credentials also went back to 1923 when he became attorney for the Bridging the Golden Gate Association.

Noplace to be seen was the name of W.J. Hotchkiss. "God" had disappeared. He could and probably should have been named as a director from San Francisco, but he was already not very popular with the Supervisors. He also could have been named from Del Norte County. However, his power base in the county was waning. He eventually lost his control of Hobbs Wall along with any hope of representing the county.

The letterhead of the Association named the five members of the executive committee and identified W.J. as Chairman of the Executive Committee. The same letterhead also identified Thomas Allan Box as Chairman of the Association. It was he who signed the correspondence in that capacity. Emma Hotchkiss collected newspaper clippings. On every one that identified Box as Chairman, she arrogantly crossed out the word. There was room for only one chairman in Emma's world.

Box was from Marin County. A local newspaper printed an article about him at the time of celebration of completion of the bridge:

MAN, WHO GAVE IT, ALL BUT FORGOTTEN

"Today's Golden Gate Bridge celebration has its 'forgotten man.'
That man is the late Thomas Allen Box, Marin county civic leader, who gave many years of his life to the creation of a public demand

for a span across the entrance to San Francisco Bay.

"Box first brought forth the idea of a bridge across the Golden Gate in 1896 in conversation with William Kent, then Congressman for Marin County, for whom Kentfield was later named. In casual conversation Box broached the subject. The congressional representative welcomed it.

"In the years to follow Box became known as 'that crazy old man' who wanted to bridge the Golden Gate. Everybody, except Box and a few others, knew it could not be built. But Box and his few kept talking the bridge until people finally began to listen to them.

"...But with the goal accomplished, Box was forgotten. He was not a politician. And when the directors were named his name was not among them. Although he was responsible, perhaps more than any other man, for the preliminary work to the erection of the mighty span, when the honors were passed around, when the work really began, he was ignored.

"His family, his wife, his sons, say that his neglect broke his heart and brought about his death February 23, 1934."

In reality, the power base for W.J. Hotchkiss (and for Box) was the Bridging the Golden Gate Association which completed in 1928 its mandate to promote the establishment of the new Golden Gate Bridge and Highway District. It was an incredibly difficult job. W.J. was there at the beginning, and he was there at the successful ending. He did his job well. Others took over and seized the glory. The final irony is that W.J. died in 1936. He was not able to see the final fulfillment of his dream.

All of the directors received a card that permitted them to drive across the bridge free for their lifetime. Nobody ever charged W.J. Hotchkiss for crossing the bridge either.

CHAPTER 21

THE KING IS DEAD

W.J. Hotchkiss died November 2, 1936 at the age of seventy-eight. The elegant eulogy by an unknown author was printed and has been preserved. Naming the decedent "Joe" rather than "W.J." suggests somebody outside of the family, probably from Sonoma County.

Whoever wrote it surely and lovingly described the man you have seen in earlier chapters. W.J. had vision and imagination. He cared for people, and they responded by caring for him. He understood how to run a business, yet his greatest business skill was the ability to choose his lieutenants. Some family members said that he just played the game of business. He liked to win, but he didn't mind losing. They did not know him as well as they thought. In the midst of his greatest business successes, he hurled himself into a tough political arena, working for the golden gate bridge. He was following his vision into a difficult and sometimes ugly fight. It was definitely not play.

W.J. would have been ideally suited to be president of a large corporation today. He would have demanded and chosen competent men to be his executives and run the day to day operations and report to him. His work would have been to put together everybody's thoughts and plans and then add his own soaring imagination. Then he would boil it all down into a plan that was workable and then start selling the plan. Through it all he would never lose his sense of humor and his love for his fellow man.

W.J. was born in the wrong era. If he had been born in 1911, he would have been forced to see what can happen to an empire that is financially overextended. Carried away by his visions in the 1920's, he expanded too far and too fast. Still, the kindness and humor and the love for his fellow man were always there.

Following is the entire printed eulogy:

There shall succeed a faithful peace;
Beautiful friendship tried by sun and wind
Durable from the daily dust of life.

William Josephus Hotchkiss-always "Joe" in the loving thoughts and on the lips of friends-was indeed "durable from the daily dust of life". His was a spirit touched to fine issues. His memory and his influence will live.

Friendship-it is the first quality that comes to mind when this splendid Californian is estimated. Throughout a long and busy life he drew to him friends from among all sorts and conditions of men. In the professions, in his favorite clubs, and in the large circle of his business peers, he is not more deeply mourned than by a host of workers in lumber camps, in packing houses, and on the farm. Joe Hotchkiss had a fine gregarious instinct. He collected friendships, just as the lover of books collects rare volumes.

His was a career of many achievements, yet from first to last his roots were in the soil. Successful master of many productive enterprises, his heart and his dearest interests had to do with land and the farming of ground. He was a striking example of the many important American business men developed from a farming background. His youth knew all the travail, the long hours, the monotony of labor, indeed all the stern demands that have to do with seed time and harvest. And whatever his many other interests his heart's desire was fully satisfied only when the land yielded its increase to his efforts. This was his major happiness in the closing years, just as it had been in the days of his youth. By this contact his character had been formed; this contact, moreover, in some subtle way, stimulated his imagination throughout the decade of his manifold activities.

That Joe Hotchkiss was a man of strong imagination all who knew him will agree; he could not, otherwise, have carried to fruition so many and such various projects.

Imagination! It was the strong stirring of imagination within him that led him years ago to visualize a bridge across the Golden Gate. To many with less vision it seemed an impractical idea in which a man usually wedded to practicalities was indulging himself. It provided the theme for much good-natured badinage. Behold, at a ripe age, the Doer has become a Dreamer! Joe Hotchkiss smiled with these joking friends-he had the gift of smiling a great deal-and steadily pursued his way. It was a long way of many obstacles. The dream came true. The empire of the north has been linked to the metropolis of the central Pacific Coast and to the empire of the south. Joe Hotchkiss, the pioneer of the

Golden Gate span, claimed no credit-and received little, except from a few whose memories are not careless. Such is the fashion of a world he understood. He was content.

This was to Joe Hotchkiss a special adventure, a bold and successful attempt to mold the future of the West. Ordinarily he found his adventure in constructive business, planning with courage and executing with the certainty that came of accumulated experience. It is not necessary to review the details of his business life. It is much more to the purpose to recall that Joe Hotchkiss won and never lost the affection and the fidelity of the many who worked with him and for him in high and humble station.

He had the gift of homely and direct expression, a gift conferred at times upon those who spring from and work the land. Humor at once dry and rich enlivened his conversation. He was a happy man, so there was much laughter in him. And his tolerance was broad. He is remembered by those who confronted him with an opinion to which he did not assent as pausing, tapping his fingers thoughtfully on desk or table, and saying "Mebbe so, mebbe so."

Conspicuous among his virtues was a zeal of helpfulness. His wisdom was freely given to others, for he liked to see men strive worthily, and was delighted to assist them to the goal. If he ever asked a favor in return, it must have been a simple one. He gave; he did not exact.

Of the loved ones that survive him this is not the place to speak. For their eventual consolation in his passing there will be the undying recollection of one who loved them, cherished them, and showed them by example the contentment that comes from integrity, from honorable living, and from warm-hearted understanding of the fellow-man.

Many of his life-long business associates and social cronies went before him. There were giants in the group, men who made history for the Pacific Coast, but he was the inferior of none of them. Those who survive have recollections to be cherished. Younger men live long under the summer shadow of his vital inspiration.

Truly, Joe Hotchkiss is one who "leaves behind a wholesome memory on the earth". He has earned the right to rest in happiness and peace.

That is the prayer of those who love and miss him.

Frank Crusius (Helena's father)

Helena (Crusius) Hotchkiss

Marius at Lick High School

Medals won by Marius at Lick

Form 1040A
U.S. INTERNAL REVENUE

INDIVIDUAL INCOME TAX RETURN
FOR NET INCOMES OF NOT MORE THAN $5,000
For Calendar Year 1921

FILE RETURN WITH THE COLLECTOR OF INTERNAL REVENUE FOR YOUR DISTRICT ON OR BEFORE MARCH 15, 1922

Or for period begun Jan 1, 1920, and ended Dec 31, 1921

PRINT NAME AND ADDRESS PLAINLY BELOW

Name: M W HOTCHKISS

Post office: KNIGHTSEN County: CONTRA COSTA State: CAL.

Do not write in this space
FIRST PAYMENT $
(Cashier's Stamp)
CASH CHECK M.O.
Examined by

OCCUPATION, PROFESSION, OR KIND OF BUSINESS: Ranch Manager

INCOME.

1. Salaries, Wages, Commissions, etc. (State name and address of person from whom received.)
   Wages + Board (w) Hotch 8 F — 3425 ... $3425 —
   Supt Rec 799 ... " ... 300 ... 300 —
2. Interest on Bank Deposits, Notes, Mortgages, and Corporation Bonds ... 120 —
3. Income from Partnerships, Fiduciaries, etc.
4. Rents and Royalties
5. Profit (or loss) from Business or Profession (not including income from partnerships)
6. Profit (or loss) from Sale of Real Estate
7. Profit (or loss) from Sale of Stocks, Bonds, etc.
8. Other Income
   (a)
   (b)
9. TOTAL INCOME IN ITEMS 1 TO 8 ... $

DEDUCTIONS.

10. Interest Paid (not including interest deducted above) ... $120
11. Taxes Paid (not including taxes deducted above) ... 45
12. Losses by Fire, Storm, etc.
13. Contributions Automill expense ... 365
14. Bad Debts (not including bad debts deducted above)
15. Other Deductions Authorized by Law Wife + Child ... 2900
16. TOTAL OF ITEMS 10 TO 15 ... 3420.00
17. TAXABLE NET INCOME (Item 9 minus Item 16) ... $439 —

COMPUTATION OF TAX.

18. Net Income (Item 17 above) ... $
19. Less Personal Exemption and Credit for Dependents
20. Balance (Item 18 minus ...
21. Tax Due (4% of Item 20)
22. Less: Tax Paid at Source
23. Income and profits taxes paid to a foreign country or possession of the United States
24. Balance Due (Item ... and ...)

17 55

Marius' 1921 income tax return

Berkeley home of Marius Hotchkiss about 1936

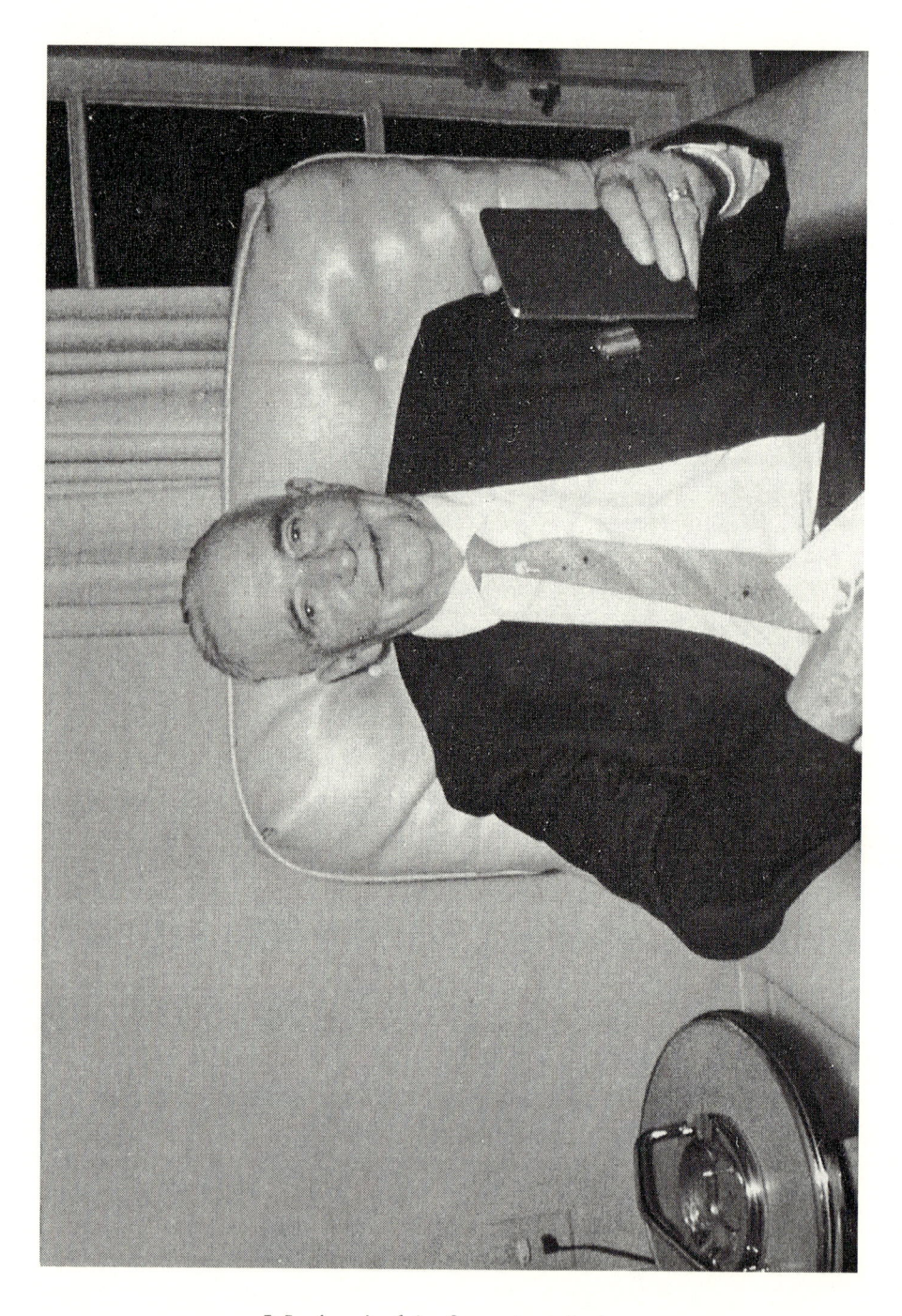

Marius in his favorite chair

Marius and Helena at baseball game.

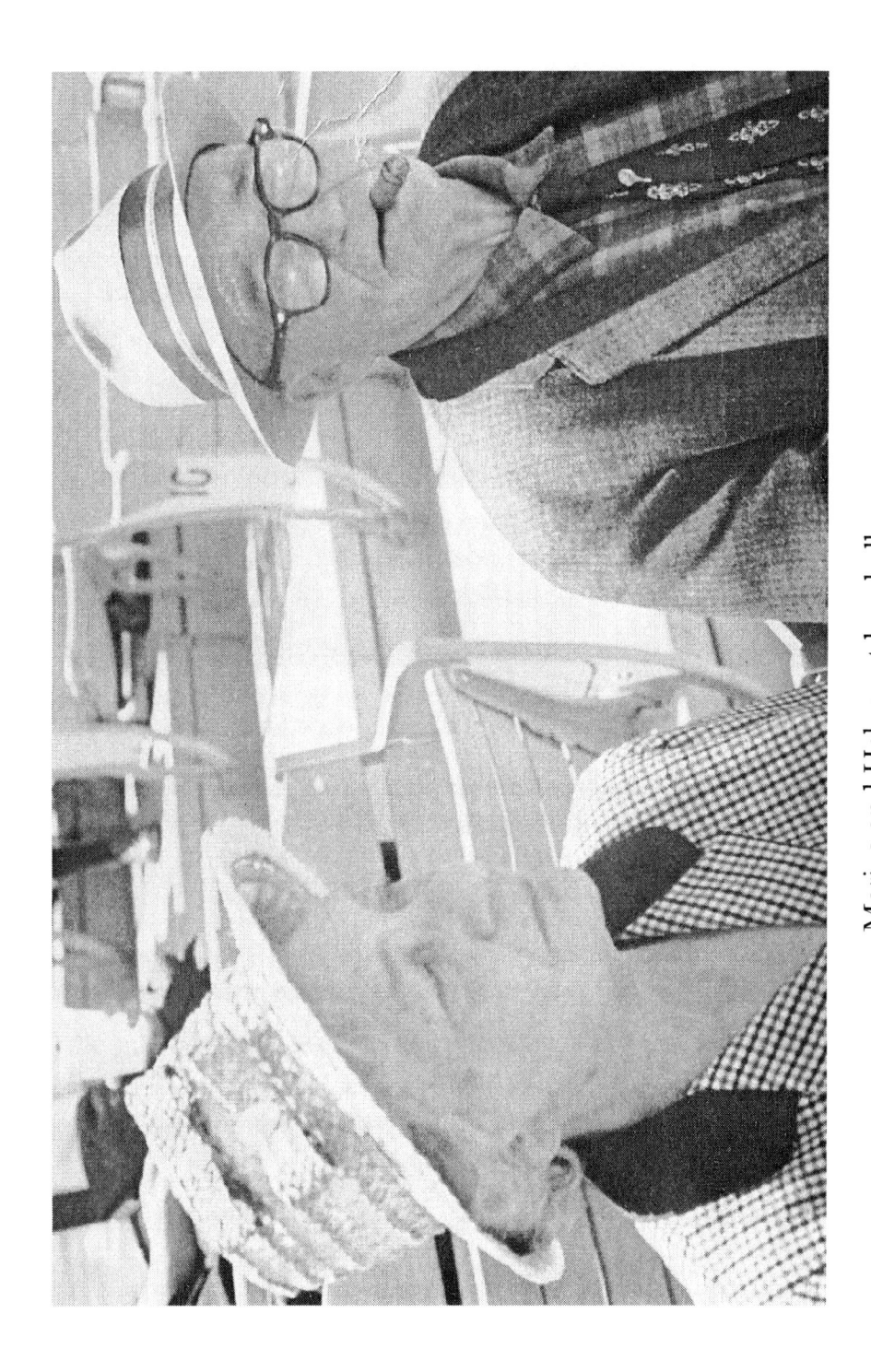

Marius, Hazel and J. Miller

Marius' dog, Cobina, was pound for pound the fiercest of jungle beasts. She sat in Marius' lap at the bridge table, fully prepared to attack anybody that was a threat to Marius. At all times she would never allow anybody but Marius to come near her. Helena was responsible for feeding. Once, Cobina literally bit the hand that fed her.

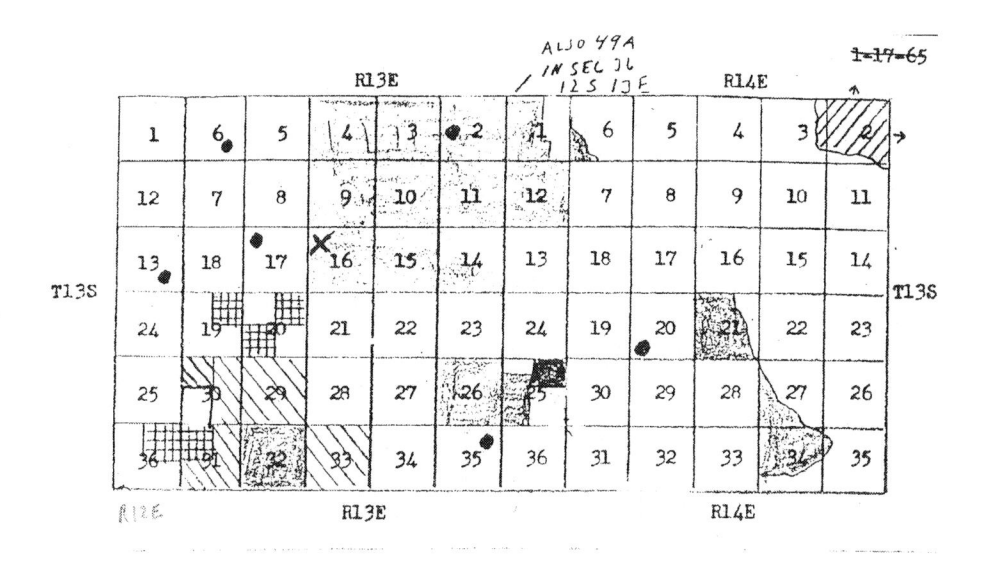

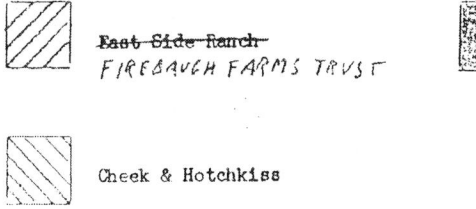

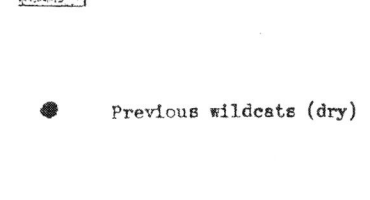

Mineral rights map originally prepared by Miller Hotchkiss

Helena and Miller

Miller and Helena

Miller as a child

Group, class of 1922 at Iron House School in Knightsen. Miller Hotchkiss front row left.

Miller Francis Hotchkiss

Miller F. Hotchkiss, portrait

CHAPTER 22

LONG LIVE THE KING

Miller Francis Hotchkiss was born November 27, 1910. His early life offered little hope for success in later years. He was the child of a world champion neurotic and a mother who had the absolute minimum of maternal instinct. Often asked to choose one parent over the other when they fought, Miller had no idea which way to turn. He turned off his emotions as well as he was able and went the route alone, powered by his amazing intellect.

Miller was sent to military academy rather than public high school. Too intelligent to get into trouble, he found the little ways to show his defiance. After dinner all the boys were required to go to the library and study. Miller studied, but not on his schoolwork. He took the opportunity to read the encyclopedia from beginning to end. This heresy proved very helpful in later life. He knew an awful lot about a lot of things.

Graduation from the University of California in engineering did not come at the best time. It was 1932, and jobs were hard to find. Following his pattern of aloneness, Miller chose to be a farmer. He asked his grandfather for capital to get started. W.J. recognized the ambition and the willingness to work hard. He loaned Miller two hundred dollars, which was soon repaid. Miller's career as an independent farmer had begun. I doubt if Miller even bothered to ask Marius for money.

It wasn't easy to make a living in the San Joaquin Valley at the time. Miller was an inveterate record keeper, leaving a trail in writing of the results of his endeavors. His first balance sheet as of January 1, 1934 shows the single asset, five hundred dollars worth of personal property. Unfortunately, that was more than offset by nine hundred and ten dollars of accounts payable. The two hundred dollars had disappeared and taken a few more dollars with it.

Time sort of heals wounds. By the end of the year 1934, there was a cash savings account of two hundred dollars, and accounts payable had been reduced to seven hundred. Net worth was still a negative fifty dollars. It would have been positive net worth if Miller had not reduced the questionable value of personal property to four hundred dollars.

The net worth took off to six thousand dollars at the end of 1935 and sixteen thousand at the end of 1936. The balance sheet had started to grow crops. There were line items for East Side Ranch, Cotton Farms and Columbia Ranch. They were joined a little later by Hay Ranch, Tule Ranch and Asparagus Ranch.

Miller also worked for the Hotchkiss Estate Company. He was employed as an assistant manager under Andre Fourchy. After W.J. died in 1936 he received a special management bonus of fifty shares of Hotchkiss Estate Company stock. This was probably for cumulative past performance. Andre Fourchy got two hundred shares at the same time.

There is no question that W.J. knew about Miller and what he had done.

Intuitive about personnel to the very end, he called his twenty-five year old grandson to his deathbed and gave him instructions on how to manage things and deal with J.M., Linville, and Marius.

Miller told me some of what W.J. told him, "Linville is never to be permitted to manage anything. Marius is never to have any money."

Miller never told me what W.J. said about J.M. (my father). I believe it would have been something like, "J.M. is kind, caring and loyal. He is the perfect man to run the precatory trust to take care of my debts of honor, but I am not entirely sure of his management ability. You should watch him."

The new king had begun his own climb to the top. He also had been given what he did not know was an impossible assignment.

W.J. had done what he could. He died reluctantly. His last words, like Michelangelo's, were, "There was so much more that I wanted to do."

CHAPTER 23

HOTCHKISS ESTATE COMPANY

We called ourselves the ten grandchildren of W.J. Hotchkiss. I was the tenth, born January 16, 1927. Gaga usually lined us up in descending order of height in front of what we called "the big house". Then we received immortality by photography.

We also had somewhat of a sense of togetherness that contrasted with the aggressiveness and competitiveness of the generation before us. We still had our differences, some of them serious, but our general atmosphere was unlike the heavy fighting for favor of W.J.'s children. They were like the Kennedy family. They got along, but everybody wanted to be first. Calling ourselves the ten grandchildren was our way of distancing ourselves from our parents. In the process we tried to develop common bonds, not always succeeding but at least trying.

Back two generations, W.J. and Gaga saw their world begin to crumble with the onset of the Great Depression that was triggered by the stock market crash of 1929. Nobody had told W.J. that leveraging investments with a large amount of debt had both risks and rewards. Things went very badly for W.J. His ability to leverage with borrowed money turned on him. He had a very high debt ratio in combination with reduced or eliminated income from the investments. Using realistic values for his equity, he had negative net worth. His empire was in danger of being destroyed.

He was still brilliant, and he was nimble. That's why the Hotchkiss Estate Company was formed. The meeting of Jan. 6, 1931, was called to order, and W.J. Hotchkiss presented his offer subject to obtaining a permit from the State Department of Corporations. He proposed that 5,000 shares of stock be issued, 800 to W.J., 800 to each of his four living children and 1,000 to Emma, his wife. This was all subject to his getting the state permit, which was received a month later.

Into the pot in exchange for those shares W. J. threw in the Firebaugh Ranch the home ranch in Sonoma County, the Napa county ranch, and his home in Berkeley. Each property was subject to various amounts of secured debt. What he did was transfer possible wealth from any increase in value of the real properties to his children and his wife.

He probably didn't transfer in all his debts nor did he transfer in all his properties. The main point is that the permit was acquired, and the assets were transferred. W.J. became president with J.M. as vice president, Andre Fourchy as Secretary and Loretta Fourchy as Assistant Secretary. The five directors were W.J., Andre and W.J.'s three male children. The authorization to draw checks showed where the power was in the company. It was authorized for W.J. alone or J.M. working with Andre, two signatures required, or it could be J.M. with Loretta.

Who were Loretta and Andre Fourchy? Loretta was a very interesting lady. She was secretary for W.J. and had been secretary for some time. W.J. thought the world of her. Her husband Andre was working in a bank in Alameda, not a terribly high position. What W.J. needed was somebody to go to Firebaugh and run the ranch, which was the key property for the future. There were two questions. Would Andre be capable of this? The decision reported by Loretta was yes he would. The second question, was Loretta, a city person, willing to go to Firebaugh with Andre? Loretta gave the answer to that also. Once more W.J. had reached into nowhere and plucked out the quality manager that he needed. Andre and Loretta lived on the ranch in Firebaugh for about 10 years before they moved to Fresno, where Loretta could resume city living. Andre then commuted from Fresno to Firebaugh, a journey of less than one hour.

Fairy tales can come true. Hotchkiss Estate Company survived and triumphed over its lifetime of twenty-three years. Farming in the San Joaquin Valley was a good business in those years. Miller Hotchkiss graduated from college in 1932 and borrowed two hundred dollars from his grandfather to get started in farming. That was the start of his personal fortune. Marius formed a partnership with Herb Cheek and managed somehow to make a profit for a few years.

Marius explained it to me, "Anybody could make money in the valley in those days. All you needed was two hundred dollars for capital. You borrowed the rest from the bank. When the crop came in, you paid off the bank and pocketed the rest."

It was not that easy for Hotchkiss Estate Company. Progress was initially very slow, but the company survived until its explosion of profitability in the 1940's. From the vantage point of the later years it was too easy to build folklore about how and why the company was formed. It was said that W. J. deliberately formed the company to hide his assets from his creditors. This is not entirely true because the Hotchkiss Estate Company was formed quite openly and legally. The other thing he did simultaneously was transfer some of the assets to his children. It is reasonable to want to provide a foundation that your children can use to make their own success in life.

The other piece of folklore is absolutely true. I would have done it myself in his position. W.J. was 73 years old at that time, looking for security as his empire was somewhat crashing around him. The arrangement that he made, the folklore said, was that he would put all his good assets into the company and the company would take care of him for the rest of his life. In other words the company would pay his personal bills and make sure there would be no foreclosure on his house or anything like that. It was done completely openly. The gambit that was used was that W. J. was given a salary by the Hotchkiss Estate Company. The salary for 1931 when the company was first formed was $12,000. This was to be his annual salary subsequently. In the December, 1931 meeting it was mentioned that business had been so rotten that he was foregoing his salary for the year 1931 but he hoped that business would be better for 1932. He did not forgive his 1932 salary.

On the surface there was nothing wrong with what W.J. did. He put some assets and some liabilities in the Hotchkiss Estate Company. Looked at from his point of view, he was providing for his own future to be comfortable in his last few year of life. He was buying time for the assets of the Hotchkiss Estate Company to produce so that his other obligations could be paid off. If he had lived another five or ten years, perhaps everybody would have been very happy, because of the continued prosperity of the Hotchkiss Estate Company. Unfortunately he died in 1936. His estate was a net loser because the liabilities exceeded assets.

The minute book of Hotchkiss Estate Company includes a description of the properties that W.J. transferred to the company:

PARCEL 1: BROADWAY RANCH (Near Firebaugh in Fresno County)

Approximately 5,046 acres owned in fee subject to a mortgage of $175,000.00 payable in annual installments of

$25,000.00, next payment due in 1932.

Approximately 4,732 acres being purchased under various contracts, total purchase price being $311,867.16 of which unpaid portion of $165,978.58 is payable in installments of from one to nine years.

PARCEL 2: "HOME RANCH" – SONOMA COUNTY

540 acres more or less of highly developed fruit and general ranch land near Healdsburg in Sonoma County, California with ranch buildings and other improvements and machinery and equipment, and including growing crops – subject to a mortgage of $50,000.00

PARCEL 3: NAPA COUNTY RANCH

Approximately 1,091 acres of fruit land and other cultivated land near Yountville, California.

PARCEL 4: BERKELEY PROPERTY

Approximately 324 feet of frontage on Claremont Avenue, Berkeley, running thru to Domingo Avenue with an average depth of 820 feet. Subject to a mortgage of $10,000.00.

STOCK TO BE ACQUIRED:
340-1/2 shares Visalia Orchard Company.

In 1931 through 1936 it would be reasonable to assume that there would be other creditors insinuating themselves into the picture with W.J. still scrambling to avoid having his empire crash. So, in Aug. 1931 the Hotchkiss Estate Company agreed to assume W.J.'s obligation of 66,500 dollars to Canadian Bank of Commerce. On Sept. 24 Hotchkiss Estate Company bought from W.J. 50 bonds of Hobbs Wall Company. Also they paid for the bonds by assuming W.J.'s obligation of 40 thousand dollars to Henry C. Hagensen. The Hotchkiss Estate Company delivered its note for 40,000 to Hagensen due in 5 years, secured by the Hobbs Wall Bonds and a deed of trust on the Napa property. At that time the bonds were probably not worth anything.

Surely thereafter there could be nothing more. Then on December 30, 1931, Hotchkiss Estate Company accepted W.J.'s offer to sell to the company 495 shares of West Side Cotton Credit Corporation, a corporation formed to finance cotton grown on the West Side of the San Joaquin Valley. The price was 102 dollars per share or 50,490 dollars. It offset W.J.'s open account of 66,500 dollars plus all the odds and ends on the books of Hotchkiss Estate Company. On that same date, the company bought 6.1 acres outside of Healdsburg for 1,000 dollars per acre, also offsetting W.J.'s open account.

Does anybody remember the gold standard? In April, 1932 Hotchkiss Estate Co. asked the Corporation Commissioner to approve solicitation to ask selected bondholders for extension of maturities on W. J. Hotchkiss Ranch First Mortgage Serial Gold Bonds issued 1923. This was just another effort to postpone debt maturity to stay afloat.

> 5-4-32 Similarly, San Joaquin Light and Power defers collection of power bills for the year until 12-15-32. (Covered by notes issued by WSCCC and guaranteed by HE Co.)

> 7-29-32 Again, Provide security for 47,836.52 owed to Canadian Bank of Commerce by deeds of trust on 3 parcels comprising the Berkeley home.

> 1-30-34 Here is a helping hand from the government. Agree to contract with U. S. Secretary of Agriculture to lease them bottom land and have it retired from production i.e. limit production and raise price.

> 8-20-34 Refinanced one of the Berkeley parcels for 10K. Corporation takes over the earlier debt.

At last came the good news at the end of the year 1934, a dividend of one dollar per share (on 5,000 shares). The directors switched to a monthly payout of twenty-five cents per month in 1935, which was repeated in 1936.

W.J. died in 1936. He was replaced on the board by Miller. J.M. became president with Linville as vice president. A bonus of 2,500 was paid to Andre Fourchy.

The 1937 dividend was doubled to fifty cents per month, which continued through 1944. Additional dividends were also paid. The first one was in the form of a note for fourteen dollars a share plus interest from 1937 to 1942. It seemed as if there was tremendous pressure from stockholders for dividends. The solution when cash was not readily available was to postpone payment and earmark future cash for dividends.

Marius and Linville were the two directors who lobbied loud and hard for dividends. The other three directors were against excessive payouts, but they acquiesced for the sake of harmony. It was not that simple. I remember when the board meetings were held at my father's house. I was a teenager living at home in a two story house. The words and the cigar smoke climbed the stairs without resistance. The yelling and screaming, mostly by Marius, were bad enough, but the addition of smoke made matters insufferable. My mother took to her room and locked the door. Opening my bedroom window helped mitigate the noise, but it pulled up the smoke simultaneously. Miller was the only one who did not smoke. I should have told him years later that I was the one who saved him from the worst effects of second hand smoke.

The good times had come. Dividends were paid. It was cash to burn a hole in his pocket for Marius, but it was opportunity for careful investment for Miller.

In later years Miller summarized the issue for me, "Your father should not have given in to Marius on dividends during the war years. He had to pay wartime income and excess profits taxes at the rate of ninety-one percent to get the dividend money. He should have used most of the money to make tax deductible improvements to the ranch."

J.M. was a kind man who, as the oldest son of W.J., was doomed to referee the family arguments. To the extent that he could, he helped Miller and also Homer's daughter, Emmy Lou. Miller respected J.M., and was unwilling to take any action against him.

CHAPTER 24

NICE GUYS FINISH LAST

In the early years the minutes of Hotchkiss Estate Co. were brief. All of the yelling and screaming were edited out. Long discussions were sometimes labeled, but they were never recorded verbatim. Likewise, anything nice that was said also hit the cutting room floor. Bare bones, that was it. There is only one exception in the minute book. The minutes of the meeting of September 19, 1945, were taken and transcribed professionally. The meeting was held in the law offices of De Lancy C. Smith. The meeting began ominously:

J. Miller Hotchkiss: The meeting will come to order. I would like to make the briefest speech in the President's seat that has ever occurred at a meeting. I tender my resignation to take place at the pleasure of the Board.

Andre Fourchy was elected president to succeed J.M. There was no hostility at the meeting. After the stunning resignation, Marius even nominated J.M. to be vice president. Andre made two separate speeches during the meeting. The first was a general statement of the problem and what he intended to do about it. The second was totally personal, an emotional tribute to J.M.'s past performance:

Mr. Fourchy: I am very happy to accept this office, and I want to thank all you people here for the confidence you have shown in me, and I am going to perform to the very best of my ability, and I am going to exercise the authority long ago exercised by the President of the Company.

We are in a tough spot now; I think we can pull it out; I have every confidence we can pull it out, and I am hoping that it will not be very long before we will be back where we started, and we will have all of this behind us, and that we will be in no worse shape than we are right now.
That is all I have to say at this point.

Mr. Fourchy: May I say just a word here? We have discussed this thing – we'll be informal for a minute. It is like I expressed it last night. It is my desire to have Mr. J.M. sit in here on this job as Vice

President, and I want to express for myself and for the rest of you, the appreciation of the years of effort that he has put in here, and the accomplishments. You will remember when we were up against it, when we had a bond issue out, when J.M. went down and refinanced that, when we couldn't see how we were going to meet the amortization. I can relate any number of things, and it would gratify me to see Mr. J.M. Hotchkiss carry on here as Vice President in the capacity that I could lean on his advice and experience. It would be helpful to me.

What was going on? What had happened? You have to go back to the beginnings. When the company was formed, W.J. put in most of his assets and some of his liabilities. Liabilities that were not included were loans from several banks. The banks formed a consortium in 1945 to sue for collection of the debt. A trial was held, and testimony was given.

Years later Miller told me that the banks had a difficult case to prove. Their main motivation in initiating the suit was to establish a bad debt in their own records. Hotchkiss Estate Co. had made money and had a fair balance sheet even after paying the dividends that Marius had demanded. The suit could probably have been settled for ten cents on the dollar. Paying that amount could have been managed easily.

If you have read this far, you probably suspect that the shenanigans that went on in 1931 were on the edge of fraud. J.M. was there at the time. He knew that there had been fraud. He fought the case all the way, blinded by the noble desire to protect his father's good name.

My mother explained it to me at the time, "Your father wanted to protect his father's good name. He bet that they would not put Tom Jones on the stand. When they did put him on the stand, the case was lost."

I remember before the trial was over my father became afraid that they would subpoena W.J.'s old records. He came home one night with his car filled with heavy file transfer boxes. It became my job to carry those boxes up three flights of stairs from the garage to the attic. I still remember every step of that journey. Mercifully, I have forgotten how many times I made the trip. Thinking back on it, I am sure there must have been more than two or three boxes. I think he made more than one delivery. It is obvious that the lawsuit weighed heavily on my father emotionally. It also weighed heavily on me physically.

De Lancy Smith, the attorney, was an old friend. He was always known by the initials D.L. He lived within a stone's throw of the Hotchkiss property in Berkeley. That could have been a bloody disaster, because D.L. was mad enough to throw a few stones. J.M. had not only lied on the witness stand, but also he lied to D.L. My mother told me that D.L. wanted to have my father sent to jail at the age of sixty-four.

Tom Jones was a Hotchkiss family cousin who worked for W.J. as a high level gofer. W.J. would send Tom to evaluate properties and deal with special problems that arose in operating properties. Tom was a good man, quite intelligent and also quite honest. I met him once and liked him. Apparently he knew too much about the formation of the Hotchkiss Estate Company. It was very shortly after Tom's testimony that the meeting of the Hotchkiss Estate Company occurred. Resignation as president by J.M. was at D.L.'s insistence. He had decided that he had to continue representing the company as their attorney, but he did not have to represent J.M. In fact at the next meeting J.M. was forced to resign as director and vice president.

The meeting of Hotchkiss Estate Company continued for quite a while. They discussed the opportunity to settle the case currently and talked about negotiation strategy.

The next meeting was also held in D.L.'s office December seventh. At the meeting J.M. resigned as director, and D.L. was elected director in his place. This was apparently part of the settlement agreement. It was then time to arrange to pay the settlement. A loan from American Trust Company had been established as four hundred thousand dollars at four percent interest. It was a first mortgage on all of the company's commercial property.

That was a lot of money at that time. To put the loan amount in perspective, note that Fourchy's salary as president was twelve thousand dollars a year. A few years later I came into the job market at two hundred dollars a month. My ambition was to be equivalent to middle managers at Chevron and Kaiser, who earned about five hundred dollars a month.

The company's setback was not fatal. The monthly dividend of fifty cents was reinstated the following year. D.L. resigned as director, and J.M. was installed in his place. Although J.M. was never again involved in active management of the company, he did manage to have the quarterly meetings at his home. Surely this move was supported by Marius, who only had to cross the street to attend the meetings. The fighting resumed, but it was not reported in the minutes. Profit was so large in the year 1947 that they declared a special dividend of forty dollars a share in addition to the regular one dollar per month. To his everlasting credit, J.M. voted "no" on the dividend resolution. Similar but slightly smaller dividends were declared in the following few years. The good times kept coming. Would they ever stop?

CHAPTER 25

DISTRIBUTION OF STOCK IN HOTCHKISS ESTATE COMPANY

In January, 1931 W.J. established the original distribution for the proposed 5,000 shares of stock to be issued, 800 to W.J., 800 to each of his four living children and 1,000 to Emma, his wife. The stock was issued. Equality among the living children was established, but it didn't stay that way.

The first change occurred May 1st, 1931, Emma, who had received 1,000 shares in the original distribution of stock, gave away 200 shares to each of the wives of her three sons. There is no indication anyplace that I have seen or heard of why Emma did not also give 200 of her shares to George Wightman, Hazel's husband. Nevertheless, George was omitted. There were no other changes in stock ownership until 1936. Emma and W.J. both died in that year, Emma dying July 27th and W.J. dying November 2nd.

What we had really were two deathbed transfers. Emma took her remaining 400 shares and put them into the pot, and W.J. transferred 775 shares. This was his original 800 shares less 25 shares given to Andre Fourchy in 1932 as a sort of manager's incentive plan. There were 1,175 shares, all coming in at deathbed time. Then came the fight.

All of the new stock was transferred January 2, 1937 after everybody had a chance to think about it and also fight about it. Fifty shares went to each of the four children, Hazel, Marius, J.M., and Linville, a little extra for the family members in addition to their original 800. 200 shares were given to Andre Fourchy and 50 to Miller as management bonuses. Another 250 shares went to J.M. Those were for the precatory trust. The word precatory means voluntary. W.J. said he had debts of honor that should be paid. These were all outside the Hotchkiss Estate Company, of course. J.M. was to manage the precatory trust. If successful he would pay off all of the debts of honor, which were included in a detail list. By 1937 of course the Hotchkiss Estate Company was doing quite well. Dividends flowed into the trust. Payment of the debts was accomplished and J.M. got to keep the 250 shares for his own account.

How many shares were left for the grandchildren? The answer is

475. There were ten grandchildren altogether. Hazel had five children. Linville had one adopted child, John Peter. J.M. had two children, Bill and Jim. Marius had one child, Miller. Emmy Lou was the daughter of Homer, W.J.'s fifth child, who died in 1924.

So then the debate started. When is a grandchild not a grandchild? Are some grandchildren more important than others? Does the division of assets among grandchildren treat each grandchild the same or does it follow the family lines of the parents. For example, should Linville's only child, John Peter, get the same as all of the five Wightman grandchildren combined?

The answer is a camel. A camel is defined as an animal that was put together by a committee. Division of stock among the grandchildren was one of the strangest looking camels ever. The highly compromised division started out as 25 shares to each grandchild. So Hazel's five children got 25 shares each, Bill Hotchkiss and Jim got 25 shares each. Then we come to the remaining three grandchildren, each of which was an only child. That did not seem quite right somehow. There's a little bonus in there probably equating Pete and Miller with J.M.'s two children. So John Peter got 50 shares and Miller got 50 shares.

Emmy Lou was an extra special case. In her favor she had the argument that as Homer's only heir she should be treated like Homer and not as a grandchild at all. In other words, she should have had 850 shares, just like Homer's brothers and sister. Actually, she got 200 shares. Congratulations, Emmy Lou, on your suddenly becoming eight grandchildren!

After the January, 1937 division of stock there was no change in stock holdings except for the following relatively minor events. The first were gifts to children. J.M. and Hazel adopted programs of gifting each year (not every year all the way along, but episodically) to their children. The gifts from Hazel accumulated to 42 shares to each child and the gifts from J.M. to each child totaled 50 shares. Marius Hotchkiss and Helena gave 150 shares to Miller. Linville, not having anybody to give to, didn't give.

Linville was divorced in 1938. The reasons were not financial. There were no major dividends coming out of the Hotchkiss Estate Company at that time, and the value had not skyrocketed. I don't know how Margaret put up with Linville for such a long time. He was an extreme alcoholic and a very mean individual when he was drunk. Margaret was a lady. She was a great golfer who played at the Orinda Country Club. She also did great embroidery. She was quite a natural and charming person, especially kind to me when I was growing up. She came to my wedding in 1948.

Since Linville had no money, J.M. had to carry the ball for Linville to defend Margaret's charges during the divorce, and of course it was a very difficult thing to do. I'm not privy to how well he did. He probably did pretty well. The important thing is that all this time he was helping Linville because Linville was of the family. He was also cheering for Margaret, hoping that Margaret would get more. Yet he played his role, as should someone in the fiduciary capacity, just as he played it in the precatory trust. He did his job. What Margaret got was 100 shares of Hotchkiss Estate Co. stock placed into escrow, which eventually came back to Linville a couple of years later. Margaret still had the 200 shares that had been given to her by Emma.

John Peter, always known as Pete, was a frail asthmatic youth. As Miller Hotchkiss said, he was obviously a homosexual, but he did not live long enough to really live a whole life as a homosexual. Because of the asthma he was turned down several times under the draft in World War II. They finally nailed him in 1944, as they were getting more and more desperate to have bodies in the military. The war ended a year later, but it was too late for Pete. He was given basic training in no greater hurry then anybody else. He was sent to Europe as a soldier and got into the Battle of the Bulge, which is famous in WWII history. The Germans fought back. They had been driven back and driven back but then made counter attacks. They created what was effectively a bulge in the allied lines, but they were finally beaten back. In the course of the raging conflict, Pete died. Pete's 50 shares of stock went to his mother, Margaret. Margaret in turn passed them on to Emmy Lou, I believe under Margaret's will. Margaret kept her 200 shares and her heirs benefited from the liquidation of the company several year's later.

The next event of consequence was very important for the future of the company itself. J.M. Hotchkiss died November 17, 1952. This created both an opportunity and a problem. The problem was that J.M. was the biggest stockholder, and he had a fair sized estate that included several other assets. The executors, my brother Bill and I, in conference with the attorneys decided that to get a good measure of the value of the stock of Hotchkiss Estate Company in J.M.'s estate we should sell 100 shares to the public. This was the first time in history that anybody other than Andre Fourchy held stock outside of the family. A firm named Hannaford and Talbot took over the 100 shares and sold them in the Santa Rosa and Healdsburg areas where the Hotchkiss family was well known. It helped in the establishment of the value of the stock in the J.M. Hotchkiss estate.

The big opportunity that came was for Miller Hotchkiss. Miller was by then a major factor in farming in the San Joaquin valley for his own account. Freed of the deference to J.M., he spoke and was heard by the stockholders. He said that there was going to be a farming crisis, that the Hotchkiss Estate Company was living on borrowed time in the valley and that the ranch should be sold. There was an alternate plan to obtain irrigation water by the formation of a water district, but there was a hundred and sixty acre limitation on the amount of water any individual could take. That sort of killed the deal on a ten thousand acre ranch. The subsequent purchaser of the large part of the ranch did indeed form a water district. Then he resold 320 acre parcels, 160 for a man and 160 each for a man and wife. That was probably about the minimum acreage for a successful farming operation in that area with federal water. At the time of the origin of Hotchkiss Estate Company, the water had been obtained from deep wells, but the deep wells were draining the aquifer. New wells had to go down deeper and deeper at greater and greater cost, so imported irrigation water was the answer for farmers in that area.

The decision to sell and the results of sales will be covered in another chapter. Naturally, Miller was the head of the group that controlled the liquidation process.

It is interesting to look back and see what the ownership of stock was at that time. Hazel had her original 800 shares plus the 50 share bonus that was distributed January 1937, less 210 shares she had gifted to her children for a net total of 640 shares. Her children had the 210 gifted shares from Hazel plus the 25 shares each that they had gotten in the January, 1937 distribution. They had 335 shares total, and the Wightman family as a whole had 975 shares. Linville had his 800 shares plus the 50 shares bonus. His divorced wife Margaret had her original 200 shares. So Linville's group in total came out with 1,050 shares.

Marius and Helena had the original 800 shares for Marius and the 200 gifted shares from Emma to Helena, and the 50 shares bonus for

Marius in January 1937, making the total 1050. Marius and Helena gave 150 shares to Miller leaving them with 900. Miller had the 150 shares that his parents gave him, plus the 50 shares he got as a grand child, plus the 50 shares that he earned for work performed for the company, a total of 250 shares. Andre Fourchy got a total of 225 shares as his management incentive.

J.M. had 800 original plus the 50 shares additional in 1937 less 100 gifted to his children. J.M. also had the other 250 shares from the precatory trust. Margaretta had the two hundred shares that she got from Emma, and their children each had 75. In J.M.'s estate 100 shares were sold to the Santa Rosa individuals.

Emmy Lou had her 200 shares for being the equivalent of eight grandchildren, plus the 50 shares from Margaret for a total of 250 shares.

If this was not share and share alike, it wasn't far away either. There were reasons for each gift and each transfer that was made.

Emmy Lou was the only one badly shortchanged.

CHAPTER 26

THE RAPE OF EMMY LOU

When a man writes his will, he has a lot to think about. For openers, he has to know what he owns. This can be done with the help of attorneys and accountants. If you ignore the really technical world of estate taxation, trusts, and charity, there is just one specific question. Who gets what?

When you write your will, you can name as many or as few people as you want. You can name your spouse, ex spouse, children, cousins, strangers, friends, enemies, grandchildren, and great grandchildren.

There are no limits. As a practical matter, your attorney might suggest that you are asking for trouble when you name your spouse but not your children or vice versa. Your estate could be headed for a painful trip to lawsuitland.

You can look for guidance from professionals and from the laws that have evolved to cover circumstances where there is no will. In the most common situation your attorney will tell you to be sure your spouse is provided for by some kind of trust that provides enough income to live on. All other assets are divided among the children, including the principal of the spousal trust after the spouse dies.

That sounds simple enough, but what happens when one of the children has died and has left children of his own? Should the grandchild get a full share, the same as his uncles and aunts? Or should the grandchild be considered as just another grandchild? My goodness, doesn't that sound just like the case of Emmy Lou, Homer Hotchkiss' only child?

The State of California has responded to the dilemma by stating that the surviving grandchild is entitled to a full family share. If this rule applied to the division of Hotchkiss Estate Company stock, Emmy Lou should have received one fifth of the stock that was divided after W.J. and Emma died.

Poor Emmy Lou, barely twenty-one years old, hardly had an idea of what was happening when she was declared to be the equivalent of eight grandchildren. She was pushed and pulled by forces that she had no way of understanding. It was J.M. who led the forces favoring Emmy Lou. The forces against Emmy Lou were led by Marius, who was nursing a major grudge that had really nothing to do with Emmy Lou.

Homer died August 2, 1924 at the age of forty-one. He had contracted a mysterious disease when he worked for a gold mining company in South Africa, and he never recovered from it. After Homer died Marius made one of his most stupid, crude and arrogant comments. He said he would comfort the widow. It was very obvious what Marius meant when he said he was going to comfort Edna. Surely Marius' wife did not like the comment. There was also one other person who really did not like the comment. Although Edna was from the small town of Crescent City, she was very sophisticated and had been involved individually in politics. Marius with all his crudity was definitely not a match for Edna. Edna literally cut Marius dead. Bumbling Marius would have inspired Edna to be especially cruel to him.

Marius was really not nice to Emmy Lou after that, substituting her for Edna, who soon disappeared from the family circle. When the concept was raised twelve years later that Emmy Lou was entitled to a full one fifth share of company stock, it did not sit well with Marius. He raised a major stink about it, leading to the final compromise solution that Emmy Lou was really eight grandchildren.

After the stock had been distributed, J.M. sent Emmy Lou on a trip to Europe at his expense. He also bought nice clothes for her from time to time. She was welcomed on family vacations at Lake Tahoe. He did what he could to help the girl who had ended up with two hundred shares instead of the eight hundred that she could have had.

Marius remained Marius. Thirty-five years after the stock division cousins Dottie and Emmy Lou decided to visit Uncle Marius one afternoon. Marius reported to me afterwards, "Hazel's girl and Homer's girl came to see me yesterday."

Emmy Lou was intelligent and also theatrical. When she went to the University of California, she wrote for the campus humor magazine. She told good stories and was often the center of attention at parties. Never at a loss for words, she could express herself and cover all the elements of a situation. The night that Marius died I called Emmy Lou to tell her that Marius was dead. Her response was, "Oh, poor old mean terrible nasty Uncle Marius!"

I certainly don't know how many shares Emmy Lou should have gotten. When the company was formed in 1931, no mention at all was made of either Homer or Emmy Lou. W.J. and Emma were both alive at the time, and they had plenty of opportunity to remember Homer. The properties that went into the company belonged to W.J. It was his call concerning who took ownership. On the other hand, somebody must have known that Emmy Lou deserved more, or she would not have become eight grandchildren.

One thing that I do know is that feelings of being left out remain. They fester, and the feelings become stronger. I received the following letter from Emmy Lou's husband, Sam Hanson:

11 August 69

"Dear Jim:

Enclosed is the last of a few steps towards the demise of the Hotchkiss Estate Company.

I was re-reading some of the old files and court actions and was struck by the unequal treatment of one of the heirs of the original five heirs of W.J. Hotchkiss.

Of course, I'm referring to Emmy Lou who didn't protest because of the family.

I guess all I'm saying is don't you forget her when I'm not around.

No mention to Em of this, please.

Sincerely,

S"

Five years later Marius' estate included some mineral rights underlying land in Fresno County. The land had been sold long before, but a portion of the underlying mineral rights had been retained. I wanted to sell these rights to avoid having to distribute small fractional interests to all of Marius' heirs. Mineral rights are very difficult to value, but fortunately I had ordered a professional appraisal of all of the mineral rights for which I was responsible. I asked Emmy Lou if she wanted to purchase the estate's mineral rights at appraised value, which I believed was a little bit less than their true value. Selling to Emmy Lou, I was motivated partly by the desire to be sure I had a sale and partly by the desire to do just a little bit more for the eight headed granddaughter. This was not a big deal anyway. In an estate valued at three quarters of a million dollars, an asset worth five thousand dollars is insignificant,

Later I spoke to Sam Hanson. We talked basically about the content of this chapter, with which he was very familiar. We also recalled that Emmy Lou had inherited one third of the Estate of Ethel Hotchkiss as well as one third of Marius' estate. I told him about the mineral rights and said I was sorry that I couldn't do any more. Sam evaluated the entire matter, turned quietly to me and said, "So ends the rape of Emmy Lou."

CHAPTER 27

FIREBAUGH FARMS

Liquidation of Hotchkiss Estate Company began in the year 1954. It is an understatement to say that the liquidation was well done. Miller had started it. The next thing to do was to run with it and score a touchdown. It didn't happen easily, but Miller kept it moving forward.

The inventory showed Miller at his best. The land was the easiest to count. All of the great central valley was surveyed based on a permanent marker established on Mount Diablo, an individual mountain located in Contra Costa County. The survey unit was a township. Each township is six miles square. It contains thirty-six sections, each a square mile. Each section contains six hundred and forty acres.

Townships in the San Joaquin Valley are successively numbered from Mount Diablo southward. The east-west direction is called a range. Combined with the township number, it pinpoints the exact location.

The largest holding of Hotchkiss Estate Company was in Township 13 South Range 13 East. The main ranch consisted of more than twelve sections, or twelve square miles.

The shorthand used to describe land holdings gives first the township, then the range, and finally the section number. Thus, the first section of the main ranch is identified as 13S 13E Sec 1. More colloquial is 13-13 Sec 1. Included in the photo section of this book is a little map of 13-13 that Miller drew in 1962 to help him keep track of the underlying mineral rights. A large portion of the mineral rights was retained and not sold when the land was sold. I have succeeded to management of the retained mineral rights, and I continue to use that same map.

The main ranch consisted of 7,687 acres of which 1,340 had rights to water from adjacent canals and were thus more valuable.

There were also several non-contiguous holdings. The canal land near the town of Mendota was 1,072 acres in parts of 13-14 Sec 21, 27, 34, and 35. The holding in 13-13 Sec 25 and 26 was 1,120 acres. Section 32 was 640 acres. Just to be different, there was one parcel of 160 acres that was in 16-14 Sec 15. The grand total was 10,679 acres, or almost seventeen square miles. It was a lot of land. Miller's inventory included fifteen producing water wells and eighty-five buildings, each one specifically identified on a map.

Miller managed to say and do whatever was necessary to persuade all twenty-five of the stockholders to agree to the liquidation. The unanimous consent permitted the use of a liquidation partnership. All assets were transferred to the new partnership, Firebaugh Farms. In the first few months the subsidiary, West Side Cotton Credit Corporation, was dissolved. Also the high priced canal land was sold, debts were collected, and Visalia Orchard Company stock was distributed to the partners. Cash distributions to partners were made in the amount of four hundred thousand dollars, equivalent to eighty dollars per share of former HE Co. Later in 1954 an additional 1,600,000 was distributed, making a total of two million dollars, or four hundred dollars per share of HE Co. Over the following eight years another four hundred dollars per share was distributed before the partnership completed its job.

Including Visalia orchard Company stock, each old share of HE Co. got liquidation proceeds of eight hundred dollars, a total distribution of four million dollars. Examples of who got what are:

	DOLLARS
Wightman family (five children total)	780,000
Marius and Helena	720,000
Miller	200,000

Much of Miller's work was involved in setting up plans for family members to buy unsold property. Purchasers were not forthcoming for the first seven months. There was a catch in the major income tax relief. All assets had to be liquidated within one calendar year to get the tax benefit. It was not easy to make the contingency plan that was fair to all stockholders. Happily, things turned for the better in August, and all the property was sold.

With an operation the size of Firebaugh Farms, Miller needed other managing partners. He probably could indeed have done it alone, but two additional partners would probably make the job easier and bring in additional background knowledge. It also gave the stockholders additional confidence that their interests were being watched. From the group of ten grandchildren of W.J. Hotchkiss two more that were able and willing to serve were Bill Hotchkiss and George Wightman. The youngest of the ten grandchildren was not invited to join, but I did make a minor contribution of some accounting work.

The three managing partners maintained complete communication by mail and phone. The internet was still a few decades away, but they got along well without it. They had many meetings. George flew to California for meetings that were held sometimes at Miller's ranch house in Firebaugh and sometimes at Bill's office in San Francisco. It is correct to say that they were three very intelligent people who did the complex job that they were employed to do.

It was not all business all the time. Once when George stayed at the ranch, he joined Miller in a trip to Las Vegas. While they were there they saw the performance by the very elegant strip teaser, Lily St. Cyr. Las Vegas shows were lavish even then. Lily performed her act in a glass cable car that ran on a track over the heads of the customers. During the course of her act she removed her bra and dropped it out of her car. George Wightman caught it. A year later, George donated the bra for a charity fund raiser. The notice in the program is worth repeating here:

> "Lily St. Cyr's bra was donated by Mr. George Wightman. Mr. Wightman refused to tell us where or how he received the bra. However, he did tell us that when he acquired it, it was still warm."

The most difficult property to sell was the main ranch because of its size. Suddenly, along came Miller's old friend, Phil Farrar. Phil had formed a partnership with Al Brown, who was a farmer. They bought the main ranch for over a million dollars. Their plan was to form a federal water district and resell the land in 160 acre increments with federal surface water attached.

As usual, Phil pretended he was somebody other than who he really was. Bill went to visit Phil at partnership headquarters. Phil greeted Bill warmly, explaining to him that he didn't know anything about farming. Al Brown was in complete charge of the operation. Phil said he had just put in some of the capital. During the conversation a copy of the equipment inventory was put on Phil's desk. Phil glanced at it briefly and then yelled, "Al, what's happening here? There were supposed to be three TD-18 tractors, and there are only two on this list."

Soon after the sale to Brown and Farrar, the three remaining parcels were sold to three different buyers. Liquidation had been completed. The Firebaugh Farms partnership continued in existence to collect the secured installment notes that had been taken back from purchasers. A lawsuit had been filed by customers of West Side Cotton Credit Corporation. Attorneys said several times that the suit was without merit, but it had named a sky high amount of damages. While the suit was still pending, Bill Hotchkiss totally refused to pay out most of the cash available for the partners. The suit finally got settled, and the final cash distributions to the partners in the amount of one hundred fifty-three dollars per share were made in 1961 and 1962. Liquidation was finally complete.

There is one very interesting corollary. Brown and Farrar established a tax free improvement district to finance the canals to bring in the federal water. The Broadview Water District issued bonds that were tax free but carried a coupon about equal to the going rate for taxable bonds. Each bond was secured by a lien on a specific piece of land. Miller knew that the security was solid. Each bond was only a fraction of what the underlying land had just been sold for. He issued a strong recommendation that family members should invest in these bonds. He bought a lot of the bonds himself. I bought some also, as did several other stockholders.

An unanticipated corollary was the friendship with Mel Morgan. Mel was a promising young attorney from Rhode Island, who found his way west in 1950 and entered into partnership with Louis Janin in the law firm that eventually became Janin, Morgan and Brenner. Mel did all of the work for the firm on the Firebaugh Farms job. In the process he became close friends with both Bill and Miller Hotchkiss. The two lawyers and the two Hotchkisses established a legendary floating bridge game that lasted until Miller's death in 1968. The important part of the game was the consumption of food from the deli that had been brought up to the game in Miller's suite at the Clift Hotel. When Miller was dieting, he switched from regular to diet Coke, but he still used it to wash down handfuls of cashew nuts.

Along the way I also became a close friend of Mel's. He was the lead attorney for every family business venture until his death in January, 2006. He was a great attorney, a warm human being and a true friend.

I presume that everybody who received liquidation proceeds

from Firebaugh Farms either spent it happily or invested it wisely. Of course, there was one exception. Marius Hotchkiss took his money and did not spend it. He invested, but not wisely. Welcome to the world of the Covelo Ponderosa Pine Company.

CHAPTER 28

CHEEK AND HOTCHKISS

Marius' activities in the latter half of the twenties and the early thirties remain vague. We know he had been at the Knightsen Ranch and the Mexican Ranch. We know that he spent some time in the Firebaugh area, maybe working for W.J., maybe farming on his own. We also know that he surfaced in Berkeley in 1931, when he built his home on the lot that W.J. had deeded him. See Chapter 33 for the details of home construction.

Marius and Helena went through periods of separation and reconciliation before the house was built. The desire to be comforted by a good shouting match alternated with the joys of peace and quiet. I think Helena spent some time living in an apartment that was right across the street from the "Big House". Emma introduced Helena into the Mobilized Women of Berkeley, a service organization that Emma had founded. After moving into the new house, Helena went on to become president of the organization.

Marius and Helena began to play a lot of bridge. I remember Bertha Debow, an aristocratic Russian refugee as one of the players. I never met her husband, Mischa, before he died. She lived in an apartment a block away. She smoked cigarettes in a long holder and spoke with an accent that was unforgettable to a small child. Once I was watching the bridge game when Bertha talked about washing dishes. She hated washing dishes, so she didn't wash very often. She piled dirty dishes into a laundry basin until it was totally full. Then she washed. At my tender age I was not clever enough to ask her when she washed her clothes.

Another couple that was heavily involved in the bridge game were Herb and Lucy Cheek. Herb was a tall, thin man who was similar to Marius in many ways. Although Lucy furnished the considerable inherited money that ran their household, you wouldn't know to look at her. She was a tiny little thing, quiet but loveable. Herb was more polished than Marius, but when it came to business abilities, Herb was a perfect match for Marius. Working together, the two brought the definition of incompetence to its highest level.

Marius could never belong to a men's club, because he didn't know what to say or do. Herb did not have Marius' problem. He was a member of the prestigious Claremont Country Club, where he often could be found on the porch playing dominos. He filled his days with bridge and dominos and occasionally making bad investments.

The Cheeks had four daughters. Sally, the youngest, married Hubert Mee. Hubert and Sally were friends of Miller Hotchkiss. I have also known Hubert for many years. Sadly, he died last year at the age of 92. He is the man I always turned to when I needed expert advice on negotiating oil and gas leases on properties where the family has retained mineral rights. Hubert was a professional consultant in this field until his death. He spent many years earlier working for Chevron, negotiating oil and gas leases in the Sacramento and San Joaquin Valleys.

Hubert once described Herb Cheek as a somewhat narrow minded person who lived in Piedmont, a wealthy suburb of Oakland. Hubert and Sally lived in Sacramento. Hubert took pencil to paper to show me what Herb saw as the map of California. Piedmont occupied about half of the total space. Toward the north was a little tiny pimple that was labeled Sacramento.

In typical sales of farmland in the 1950's the buyer and seller would divide the underlying mineral rights evenly as sort of an afterthought to the main sale of the land.

Miller's deals were different. He had asked Hubert's opinion and had been told that the mineral rights had good value of their own. A listing of the mineral rights percentages that Miller retained for the family on the different sales is just one more tribute to Miller's genius. Most of the percentages were 71 or 77. On one small parcel he set the record at eighty-seven percent. Many of these parcels were subsequently leased to oil and gas companies who paid cash rental. The larger percentages of ownership meant extra dollars for the family.

It was probably inevitable that Herb and Marius would form a farming partnership. The year was 1933. They were guided to property that had been used as pasture land totaling 2,560 acres. This is four full sections. It was a lot of land. Desert Ranch's 2,560 acres compare to 1,600 acres for Miller's East Side Ranch, 5,000 for Hotchkiss Estate Company's original Firebaugh ranch, and 2,300 acres of the Knightsen ranch. Marius was ready to compete with his father, his son, and his brothers.

It is a wonder that the partnership was not named Hotchkiss and Cheek. How did Herb manage to prevail over Marius in primary naming rights? Marius would not have liked to lose that kind of an argument. On the other hand, maybe the fact that it was mostly Herb's capital going in had something to do with it.

Historians are blessed with incredibly good overview records prepared by Miller Hotchkiss for his ventures. In contrast, let Miller's words explain about Marius. The following is abstracted from Miller's report prepared April 1, 1943, ten years after Marius and Herb began their operation.

"On January 1st, 1943 I assumed management of the Cheek and Hotchkiss ranch near Firebaugh. During the last three months I have been able to make certain observations and come to the conclusions which are presented in this report. The report will deal mainly with the future operation of the ranch and is therefore a complete plan of operations which is presented for your approval. Observations, conclusions drawn, and future plans are based on past records, personal observations, and opinions received from successful local farm operators.

"On January 1st, 1943 the general condition of the ranch was poor. The equipment was adequate but in need of repair, housing was poor and inadequate for the size of the operation, pumps and wells were at a low efficiency, labor conditions were poor due to lack of housing and a sub-standard wage scale. Most of the fields were badly fouled with annual weeds."

That was the analysis. The solution was simple. Miller did one thing that was not included in the written report. He told both Herb and Marius to stay away from the ranch and avoid any effort to participate in management. It must have frightened both of them. They certainly knew that their investment was falling apart around them. Miller was their savior. This was the first of several times that Miller rescued Marius from his own incompetence. Miller explained the plan to me, "Marius would never accept any suggestion that I made to him. I have to wait until he is so totally mired in a mess that he just wants to get away from it. Then he will ask me for help. I tell him that I can do it, but he has to stay away."

The written report said simply, "On January 1st arrangements were made to remedy these conditions. Satisfactory progress has been made to date and will be completed by July 1st at which time all equipment will be in 1st class condition, adequate housing in good condition will be available for the necessary employees, all pumps and wells will be at peak efficiency, all fallow fields will have had a cover crop plowed under and will be fallowed to clean up the weed condition."

Miller's report went on and on with detailed explanations of what was going to be done. It was all done and done well. It had been a good time for farmers. Even under Marius' management there was a profit of 26,000 in 1942. That amount did look somewhat puny compared to 66,000 in 1943 and 146,000 in 1947 under Miller's management. It was nice for Miller to have good accounting records to work with in the future. In contrast Miller's report on the history of the ranch says simply, "The land was first purchased and broken in 1933. Detailed records are not available as to the operations during the past ten years and all information is more or less hearsay."

In May, 2003 I had a very enjoyable conversation with Hubert and Sally Mee. Sally was somewhat ill, but Hubert was sharp as a tack in his mid eighties. My fortuitous use of a tape recorder provided a permanent record of the conversation.

Sally: My father went down to the ranch with W.J. very often.
Jim: How often did he go down?
Sally: I'd say several times a year. There's no reason to go down, nothing there.
Jim: After Miller took over, then he went down less?
Sally: After Miller took over, he never went down.
Jim: Yeah, (chuckles) he would want to go down to see Marius and see what Marius was doing, but Marius wasn't there any more.
Hubert: What was the famous story about Miller trying to do an inventory of equipment down there? They went out to the Desert Ranch, it was an old barn built of wood. Pumpkins, wasn't it?
Jim: Cantaloupe.
Hubert: Cantaloupes, and they hauled them all out in front. All the equipment was hidden underneath. It was all unreal, wasn't it? [Reference is to the large TD-18 tractor that had been totally concealed by several thicknesses of cantaloupe.]
Jim: Yeah, and Marius didn't know how to use the telephone.

Every time he needed a part for a tractor he would get into his car and drive into Los Angeles.

 Sally: Oh really.. none of the parts available locally?

 Jim: They didn't have that kind of stuff in Fresno. Fresno wasn't that close either.

 Hubert: One of the things that really amused me was how Miller got the price of power down for pumping there. Did you ever hear that?

 Jim: No, no.

 Hubert: Oh eminently, be sure I'm saying it right.. They had them captive to the great big Standard Pacific gas line that went from Kettleman Hills to the Bay Area, taking the Kettleman Hills gas and PG&E would charge you a tremendous amount for electricity for pumping charges. And so they decided that they would do something about it. I guess the way Miller told me, I wouldn't be surprised if it was Miller but it might have been Marius, went to the Public Utilities Commission and got them declared a public utility and then took the gas and used that rate to force PG&E to charge them only at the PUC rate for all their water requirements that went out of the gas pumping station. They were all alone at the free pumping stations. And they played that pretty well.

 Jim: Oh, I bet

 Hubert: Had you heard that?

 Jim: I hadn't heard that one at all. I heard Miller thought the county needed an airport someplace in his area. He suggested that he'd be glad to donate the land for the airport and the airport consisted of a landing strip, that's it, and a small hanger where Miller's plane was. The county also needed a fire station, so Miller suggested that it would be nice that they would put the fire station on his property and he would donate them the land. Same deal. And the gin, the cotton gin. Yeah sure, you guys can put the gin right on our property. We like that.

 Sally: Of course you know the story of housing the German prisoners of war.

 Jim: I don't know the details. I just know they had them.

 Hubert: Well, they had a whole bunch of German prisoners of war so they provided housing out at the ranch. They worked for the ranch.

 Sally: Where did they get the housing?

 Hubert: Well, they went to an old company way back in the hills and brought all the houses down and put up a prisoners of war camp on the ranch there. Had you heard that?

 Jim: I had never heard that.

Hubert: Well, that was pretty well documented, and then Miller wanted to build his big home at the East Side Ranch. When they built their plant there was a hell of a lot of big timbers down there. So, we got a truck and trucked all the timbers down and used that as the basis for building their home up there. You remember the ranch, don't you?

Jim: Oh yes, very well.

Hubert: Yeah, it was a beautiful home.

Jim: Yes, I remember very well. Isabel and I stayed there several times when I probated Miller's estate. We came down every week for over a year.

Hubert: I want to ask you about when Miller took over for Marius and Herb. It was with their understanding that they would have nothing to do with it. They were to keep their nose and hands out of the business and Miller would do everything, which he did eminently...

Sally: I assumed he knew that.

Jim: You know I read the detail of that yesterday again. I tried to prime myself a little bit before I came up here. I knew a lot of it and some I reviewed and a couple of things surprised me when I saw them, but I was telling Hubert earlier that Miller couldn't do anything without writing a report, and he kept his reports. So I am reading his report on Desert Ranch, and it says, " The land was broken in 1933 there are no records surviving from 1934 through 1941."

Hubert: That was the writing of Marius.

Jim: But a lot can be determined from hearsay. Then he described all the things that were wrong with the ranch, not just weeds throughout the fields but also insufficient labor force, underpaid labor, insufficient housing, equipment in bad need of repair, and of course it was interesting. He took care of all of it by July. Six months was all he needed. It was wonderful.

Sally: We have a copy of that one.

Hubert: You sent me a letter. Miller was farming the East Side Ranch then, and was he farming the Hotchkiss Estate Company?

Jim: No.

Hubert: Andre Fourchy, was doing it.

Jim: But he was farming both the East Side Ranch and Desert Ranch. Typical of Miller, he said that it took him five years to get delivery of a new tractor. This was during the time after the war. When he finally got a tractor in, Cheek and Hotchkiss paid for half of it and East Side Ranch paid for half of it. He found that particular equipment was not used at the same time on both ranches. So when it was the time to be used at Cheek and Hotchkiss it was down at Cheek and Hotchkiss working and when it was time to be used at East Side Ranch it was up at East Side Ranch working and he only needed half as much equipment.

Hubert: He was just very practical, typical engineer with a plumbing practicality.

Jim: Yes, and his cattle feedlot looked like something that Satan had thrown together, all used stuff, and he made it work.

Hubert: I was involved in that. That was when they put the feedlot in on the East Side Ranch and they went out and bought a lot of the tropical mats, landing mats they used in the South Pacific. They bought great masses of these metal flat surfaces, that would accommodate the soil and they laid those in there and they used them for trenching. They were landing mats and they would cut them up and made them pathways so they could run the cattle in the feedlot. How big a feedlot was it, do you reckon?

Jim: Hell, I have the feedlot reports, but I just haven't looked at them for a long time.

Hubert: Did they write documentation on that?

Jim: I'm sure there is. I'm sure Miller would not overlook that. So tell me, you started to tell me in the car about Herb. You said he was charming.

Sally: Impractical, loved to play dominoes or whatever. He was not a family man, but he was good, nothing wrong with him. What should I say?

Jim: He belonged to the Claremont Country Club.

Hubert: Yeah.

Sally: The live owner or the live member of the terrace club.

Hubert: The Berkeley Terrace Club.

Sally: because he had his attendance shattered during WWI, the whole town was shattered. Herb was considered to be a charming dilettante.

Jim: I love that.

Hubert: Why that's what I think about him. There was no big deal about it. He'd get himself into these bad investments, which was a thing he had.

Sally: I was too young to know too much, I'm trying to think what else.

Jim: There was probably enough money there that he couldn't make very large inroads into it anyway.

Hubert: Well you know Jim, he... I don't know how the investments are but I understand that it was Van Loben Sels heard of all this land being available for sale. They bought it from an old sheepherder friend named Arvious. He was a sheepherder from the Little Rock. And they bought the land for thirty dollars an acre.

Jim: I know this was pasture land before.

Hubert: And I assumed what Cheek and Hotchkiss bought was in addition to what the Estate Company bought. It was a big chunk of land.

Jim: Completely different, completely different. Cheek and Hotchkiss was Cheek and Hotchkiss. Estate Company was Hotchkiss Estate Company. They had different locations. Hotchkiss Estate company did have Section 32 next to Cheek and Hotchkiss. There is fascinating stuff in the files. Marius wanted to trade sections, and Marius wanted to do this, and Marius wanted to do that, and Andre Fourchy didn't want to do this and didn't want to do that. And they hung to their positions rather well and they never did trade.

Hubert: Where did Andre Fourchy come into the picture?

Jim: Andre Fourchy, well...his wife Loretta was a really good secretary for W.J. in the 1920s and Andre was working as a bank teller in Alameda and W.J. wanted somebody to run the ranch. Loretta thought it would be great to take Andre down there and make him learn how to run a ranch, which he'd be probably quite capable of.

Hubert: Do you remember Andy?

Jim: Yup.

Hubert: He always had his name in the Fresno Bee.

Jim: When my brother moved down there...

Hubert: Who is that?

Jim: Bill.

Sally: He only had one brother.

Hubert: Oh yeah.

Jim: When my brother moved down there in 1941, Andre was still living on the ranch. During the time afterwards Andre and Loretta moved into Fresno. Andre commuted and my brother took over the main ranch house. Anyway, they probably had been waiting to do that with my father pulling the strings and my brother with his little child, Bill, born in 1940. So, that was accomplished, and Loretta went into society, I believe in Fresno, and that's where you're probably hearing about her social activities.

Jim: Getting back to Herb, we know he played bridge a lot. Did Lucy play also?

Sally: They played with Helena, Marius, Lucy and Herb and somebody else.

Jim: It's funny I don't remember Lucy at all, I remember her name.

Sally: She was very quiet, and she was the one who was in the background. She was one of those people that if you knew her you loved her. She didn't know many people.

Jim: Was she tall, short?

Hubert: A little bitty..

Sally: Small, little, like my sister.

Jim: I never met any of them. I remember that Herb was a tall one.

Sally: He was 6 foot 4.

Jim: He was?

Hubert: She was about 5'1". Of course they were very good friends of Marius and Helena's. And then who were the other people, the Russians?

Sally: The who?

Jim: Debow.

Sally: I guess.

Jim: My contact would have been in 1933-34-35, maybe a little later.

Sally: Generally, the game was at Marius and Helena's house in the living room.

Jim: that's where I met them. I remember Herb had discovered something great, and he was talking about it. You remember silly things. I was a little kid, and I had never heard of this thing before, and that's why I remembered it. Herb wanted to talk about laxatives.

Sally/Hubert: What?

Jim: Laxatives.

Hubert: Oh. (chuckled)

Jim: And he explained that you don't have to take laxatives. All you have to do is drink three glasses of warm water in the morning. I was just fascinated because I had never heard of this before.

Sally: It made sense.

Jim: Right. I remember once my mother's sister, Aunt Kate, she was a baronial visitor at our house. She lived in Sacramento. She came down from Sacramento. Her two sons both worked for Dean Witter. She had been widowed long, long ago. I was just reminded of this because of the laxatives and I was just in high school then. I had a tin of laxatives in my hand, Ex Lax. I think I took it once in my life. Anyway, Aunt Kate says, "what's that?" I said, "It's Ex Lax. It's a laxative, Aunt Kate." And she said, "Well, it'll take a whole box of that to move me."

Hubert: Tell me what records did you get from Cheek and Hotchkiss when Miller ceased to be the manager?

Jim: What I acquired was the contents of Miller's desk and vault. Miller kept very careful records and I took whatever was there. Heck that was 1968, that was 35 years ago. I had the idea then that I might want to write a book about this someday, and so I just kept it stored. I didn't keep the whole thing, but I kept an awful lot. It was stored under cabinets and stuff like that. When my partner decided that I was moving out, we resurrected everything that was ever there. I took it all over to my rented quarters, and I had lots of room over there to store it. I bought two new filing cabinets besides, so it is all stowed. I have a girl who comes in one day a week and helps me with the writing. The writing projects we got all organized in alphabetical order and all that stuff.

Hubert: Sally and I were ones that were very fond of Marj and Miller. Marj and Miller were good friends of Sally's, and when I came along, they forwarded me right into it. We always had a tremendous lot of respect. Now, I didn't know much about, I didn't know anything about Fourchy and the Hotchkiss Estate Company. I only saw Marius and Helena when we would go over there and play cards or Chinese checkers or something.

Sally: and Christmas.

Jim: What can you tell me about Marj?

Sally: What can I say about Marj? I really liked her very much.

Hubert: Oh, I did too.

Sally: What else can I say about Marj? She was interesting in her own way, and I liked that. Can you think about anything?

Hubert: She told me a very funny story. She was invited to go over to Carmel and stay with a lady friend of hers, and Miller was off the ranch. She was in the living room and saw a check for five hundred dollars from the Borden Co., a special award. Marj turned to the hostess and said, "What is this all about? And she said, "I saw an announcement in one of the magazines of a literary contest extolling the virtues of the new condensed milk product. I decided to enter the thing and I received a very nice reply. Whoever was running the department program complimented me on the original verse and saying they couldn't publicize that as the winning verse but hoped I would accept the award of five hundred dollars. So Marj said she asked the hostess what was the entry. She rummaged around the desk and found the entry that went something like this:

"Borden's milk is the best in the land. It comes to you perfectly canned. No tits to pull, maneuver, or twitch, just punch a hole in the son-of-a-bitch."

Had you heard that?

Jim: No I hadn't.

Hubert: That's what Marj told me. I thought it was funny.

Jim: I see why they couldn't publish it.

Hubert: You know Miller and I used to go fishing together.

Jim: Oh really?

Hubert: We went up to King's Canyon. We would have a wonderful time. You [Sally] would stay down at the ranch with Marj and he and I would go trout fishing up there. We would have a great time together. He was really a great guy in my book.

Jim: Yes!

Hubert: I can't think about any really hurt moving encounters. It was a very friendly relationship. I do remember one thing that was very amusing. Miller and what was her name, the girlfriend?

Jim: Evi.

Hubert: Evi. They flew to Mexico in Miller's plane and they came back with a whole bunch of Mexican sweaters. Did you get one?

Jim: Oh yeah. [The sweaters were a tremendous bargain for a good quality product. Miller and Evi literally filled the plane with sweaters, which they gave to most everybody they knew.]

Hubert: I got one and Sally got one, and it was free. Miller was great. He was the fellow that got me interested in financial service for investments. It was one of the big ones. Miller made a lot of money, didn't he?

Jim: yeah. My son Ed is exactly like Miller in one way. It used to just amaze the accountant in me. Miller had a lot of money, and he did a lot of things, but they never seemed to cost him much money.

Hubert: NO!

Jim: Ed is exactly the same way. Ed is a client of my firm, HC Financial Advisors; and with just a bit of help from Dad a very few gifts plus astute financial management by HC Financial Advisors and his own hard work, add the fact that he doesn't spend anything. He gets an annual report, and every year Dianne comes to me and says, "Are you sure that Ed doesn't spend any more than that?" That's all that he spends. He lives high, he lives first class and he does all these things.

Hubert: And airplane, and fancy cars.

Jim: Yeah, Miller was exactly like that. We speak for the family.

Hubert: Oh, great, oh great, well I don't know I just uh, every memory I have of Miller is always funny. He and I used to think about lots of things. With those standards I helped Miller do oil and gas work, and I didn't expect any compensation. I just did it for the family, but I used my best judgment. I'll never forget he met me in Fresno once when I was coming from Bakersfield to Sacramento, and he says I got a present for you. What in the world have you got now? So he goes inside of his car and he has a whole big cardboard carton full of all kinds of liquor, scotch, bourbon, rum and gin. Hey, I want you to have some for Christmas. I said what's this all about? Well he says you know I don't drink and all these salesman give me presents and I just accumulate them and then give them away as Christmas presents. You heard that didn't you?

Jim: I did hear that. Yes, very practical. I remember once we went down there. You got to bring a host gift.

I said ok. It doesn't have to be much, just something thoughtful. So I bought a bunch of cocktail napkins.

Miller says thank you very much and opens the cabinet door underneath his sink, and in there were about a hundred unopened packages of cocktail napkins, and he throws it in there and closes the door.

Hubert: Oh gees. He used to get awfully mad at Herb and Marius. He told them to keep the hell out, to keep their damn hands out of the plate, and he made them lots of money.

Jim: So how much was Herb and how much was Marius? That's what I have been wondering about.

Hubert: Oh I don't know really. It was all done through checks, because they pretty much abdicated in favor of Miller.

Jim: That was a damn good thing.

Hubert: Oh shit, they were the essence of mismanagement!

Jim: Well, poor old W.J. I got the piece together pretty well now. He had Hobbs Wall from the start, so he sends Marius up there to be an assistant foreman or something and he must have driven everybody mad. I don't think he was any help.

Hubert: When was that, in the early days?

Jim: Yes. And as I said, Marius was the most erratic person I had ever met.

Hubert: Who?

Jim: Marius. He was incredibly erratic. And always primed to get the better of anybody, and almost blowing it every time, because he was either transparent or stupid in doing it. After the Crescent City affair, I'm talking about Marius and how poor W. J. had to deal with him. Marius got shifted to the Knightsen ranch, the one with the dairy.

Hubert: A dairy?

Jim: Yeah, Didn't I ever tell you about the dairy with my son? Joe's never going to be a big earner. My son is a good guy, and very conscientious about his work, and works hard, and has a lovely wife and a wonderful family.

Hubert: That's Billy Joe's kid?

Jim: That's my boy. That's my oldest, Joe. So we got this place ten acres, in Brentwood near Knightsen, where the Hotchkiss ranch was. They have a pre-fab house and a pre-fab garage and a pre-fab barn. Then, all of a sudden the fire department appears one day and says, "Mr. Hotchkiss we are trying to completely map this territory, all these homes that have been going up down here, helter skelter. We are trying to name all these streets and we are trying to preserve the history of our area as well." Joe says, "Do you have Hotchkiss?" "Yeah." "Fine, we will call it Hotchkiss Lane." So Joe's house is listed as 500 Hotchkiss Lane.

Hubert: That's perfect for that gentleman.

Jim: Yes, there's nothing wrong with it. W.J. would be smiling. If you really want coincidence, a guy who lived on Bethel Island, who has lived there for many years was writing a book about the history near Bethel Island. He knew that W. J. had the Knightsen Ranch and he got to meet me. He said, "Say there was a girl I knew a long time ago I think she married a Hotchkiss. Do you know any other Hotchkisses? I said yes. Later I introduced him to Bill's widow, Peggy.

Hubert: So where is Peggy now?

Jim: She's married to the guy, for God's sake.

Hubert: Oh my God.

Jim: She was married to Tom at that time, Tom Cox. Tom said to Peggy, when he was dying, "Well at least you got twenty years out of me." Peggy waited a year and started dating. I had already arranged for Peggy to see Bob and get back together again. The last time they saw each other was in the third grade, I think. Tom Cox sat like a Spanish matriarch supervising that luncheon and making sure nobody said anything they would regret. Of course, Bob stayed away until Tom died. It turns out that Bob was a really nice guy. He ran the irrigation district.

Hubert: Which one? The Jersey Island?

Jim: Bethel Island.

Hubert: I represent the Jersey Island.

Jim: He doesn't cover Jersey but he has the Hotchkiss Tract.

Hubert: How about the Reel Track?

Jim: No, but he has the Minutes of Reclamation District Number 799 signed by my grandfather.

Hubert: I'll be damned.

Jim: The district held its meetings at Number One Drumm Street in San Francisco.

Hubert: How long did they keep their office in San Francisco in the Visalia Orchard Company?

Jim: Well, I took it over.

Hubert: You got rid of it didn't you?

Jim: I got rid of the San Francisco office about 74-75 probably. I held Visalia Orchard Company for a while. I wasn't sure what I wanted to do, and I wanted to be sure I was doing it right. I had taken Visalia Orchard Company in as part of my management package. You know, part of my office expense was paid by Visalia Orchard Company.

Hubert: So it's still in existence?

Jim: Oh no, I liquidated it. That was the one where the stockholders couldn't get more than one and a half percent of the land value as dividends. Incidentally, I made a mistake that I will never make again. I tend to be too much mister nice guy. I just like to do things for the poor people. I am probably much like Miller in that phase, but I did something that was stupid. This lady in New York City owned single handedly about 30 percent of the stock of Visalia Orchard Company.

Hubert: Was she a Hotchkiss?

Jim: No, she was the heir of one of the two partners of W.J. that had formed Visalia Orchard Company originally. So I wrote her and said, wouldn't you like to be represented on the board? We have our meetings every January? She sent her son, John. Boy, he went to Cleone Stevens and said, "You know if we put our stock together, you can control this company." Cleone says, "No, I promised W. J. Hotchkiss that I would always vote with the Hotchkiss group. I never should have given John the opportunity. He was a nice guy, but he was a predator.

Hubert: What ever happened?

Jim: Nothing, because he couldn't get anything, and I liquidated it a year or two after that.

CHAPTER 29

COVELO PONDEROSA PINE COMPANY

"We are running more lumber right now than W.J. ever did!" When Marius said that, Miller knew it was time for him to start watching closely.

Miller explained it to me several years later. "I have to wait for him to get in pretty deep. Then he will ask me for help. If I offer help too early, he will reject it."

Marius had received three hundred thousand dollars from Firebaugh Farms in 1954. Another 60K went to Helena. It was Marius' opportunity to make some brilliant investments and show the world how great he was. Nobody really knows how Marius found the small town of Covelo. It is in the foothills of Mendocino County, the next County north of Sonoma County, the place of Marius' birth. It probably started, as always, with an undocumented loan from Marius followed by a tremendous escalation in volume.

Before the big lumber empire started, Marius had already done business in Covelo and had been sued. Miller heard about it, and he was concerned. The damages sought were not large, but Miller wanted to err on the side of caution. He told Marius that he was going to send one of Miller's attorneys from Fresno to Covelo on the trial date.

By golly, Marius triumphed over his son again. He reported to Miller that there had been no trial. The whole matter had been settled. Marius amplified further, "I didn't even use that high priced attorney you sent up there. I used the other fellow's attorney, and he didn't even charge me for it."

Marius' knowledge of the law also showed a few years earlier. He did not have large amounts of money then, but he was still able to make a few unsecured loans. Miller found out about one loan and convinced Marius to sue for collection. Miller went into court with Marius and the attorney, thereby limiting Marius' choice of attorneys. When Marius was on the witness stand, he described the loan in vague terms. The judge interrupted, "Mr. Hotchkiss, am I to understand that you loaned money to this complete stranger without security of any kind, and you didn't even take back a promissory note?"

Marius responded, "I didn't come here to be insulted!" With that, he left the witness stand and walked out of the courtroom and out of the building.

In telling the story, Miller explained that the next step was up to the judge. He could have fined Marius or even sent him to jail. Instead, the judge laughed. The case was over. Marius did not pass "Go" and did not collect two hundred dollars, but he didn't go to jail either.

Marius finally came to Miller asking for help near the end of 1954. Miller responded by offering help, but with a string attached. Marius was to put the entire Covelo operation in trust with Miller as trustee. Marius would get the ordinary income from the trust. For good measure, Marius had to toss in the remaining two hundred thousand that he would be receiving from Firebaugh Farms. This was the basic pattern that Miller used in the future. First, let Marius get in trouble and ask for help. Then Miller would bail Marius out and take the principal into a trust.

Miller was now a lumber baron, with no experience in running a lumber business. He learned quickly, and the business started to shape up. Mel Morgan helped out by setting up three separate corporations for tax savings. Morgan's plan did not work out too well. It was intended for a profit making venture, and this one really did not qualify. In addition Miller declared that he couldn't figure out what was really happening with all of those corporations involved. He wanted it kept simple so that he could grab hold of the management and know what he was doing. Covelo Ponderosa Pine Company had a lovely ring to it, implying corporate strength and power. Actually it was just a dumping ground for all of the Covelo stuff for which Miller was responsible.

Miller was able to make a profit after he got Covelo organized, but he had to fight for it. It is reasonable to expect that a large business venture established by Marius was going to have lots of problems. All the time, Miller had the entire operation up for sale. Then, as Miller explained it later, "Another Marius showed up, and I sold him the whole works."

The attorneys drew up the necessary documents including fire insurance on everything that had value along with lender's loss payable to protect the mortgages that were carried back. Less than a year later, the whole works burned down. The event was so fortuitous, that Miller insisted that every family member plus Mel Morgan record their alibi for the date of the fire. Miller was quite safe, having spent the night at Vogelsang High Sierra Camp in the middle of the back country in Yosemite National Park. You may ask if he planned that. Well, he did not.

In 1955 and 1956 the Marius W. Hotchkiss Trust was established with corpus of five hundred thousand dollars. Miller had managed to get Marius' money back and preserve it for the future of the family. He also grabbed the future distributions from Firebaugh Farms BEFORE Marius could invest them.

CHAPTER 30

MILLER AND ME

The marriage to Marj was stormy. Her father was right on when he kindly said to Miller, "Don't marry her, Miller, she's a real bitch."

Miller was quite possibly blinded by the sex. It was intense, and it was stormy. Miller told me one story about Marj. He said she was triggered by some commonplace event. He named it to me, but I don't recall. Anyway, the result was that she stormed for a while and then started throwing things. By then, they were both yelling. After a few dishes, Marj escalated to the floor lamp. The crash of the lamp was a shock to both of them. A few more words followed, and then they literally jumped into bed.

Miller was a man who learned from experience. He told me, "The next time this happened it started the same way, and we ended up in the same place, but we got there a lot quicker."

In 1931 Miller was a generation or two ahead of his time. He had difficulty understanding more than one couple, "You mean you didn't sleep with her before you married her?"

Marj's volatility became worse, and she eventually sought psychiatric help. It did not really help her. She became an alcoholic, divorced Miller, and lived an empty and hostile life. She died in 1967, a year before Miller died.

Miller had a completely different result from psychotherapy. He had gone through life with a cold and brittle personality. The new Miller exuded warmth. People who met him in the later years were really impressed with him. On the other hand, those who had known the cold Miller could not quite adjust to the new. Miller was sixteen years older than I. We had hardly said a word to each other before 1953. We were two of the ten grandchildren of W.J. Hotchkiss, but he was the oldest, and I was the youngest. I had heard stories about Miller and his icy personality, but I never got to see it. We had the common goal of helping Marius. This was the opening bond. As time passed, Miller met and liked my wife, Isabel. Evi Minor developed into a steady lady friend for Miller, and we became a frequent foursome.

Someday I hope to write in detail about those years. The concise explanation will have to suffice here. I developed a fondness for Miller. He gave me something I had really never had before. He loved me like a son, but I didn't have to do anything to earn the love. He was going to love me just the same. I worshipped him.

Miller recognized in me so much of the loneliness and fear that he had suffered as a child. He knew he could help me become stronger and more sure of myself. It was a chance for redemption for him. We were a team. I even sat in on a couple of sessions where Miller and Marius screamed at each other.

Miller thundered, "Your friend never answered my letter."

"He had an excuse," Marius replied. I saw the warning sign on Marius' face, the confident sign of a trap building. I didn't know how to warn Miller, so eventually the trap was sprung.

Miller pursued the matter, "What do you mean, he had an excuse? There is no excuse for something like that!"

"Yes, there is," said Marius, springing the trap. "He can't read or write." Triumphantly, Marius eased back in his chair.

I thought it was funny. Miller did too. His whole mood changed. He laughed and said, "Ask him to call me on the phone."

I kept track of all of Marius' cash outlays and kept Miller informed. After the 1955 trust was formed, Marius continued his lending policy. It was not difficult to find borrowers. Marius was not handicapped by having to tell the truth, so he could build himself up as a powerful figure in whatever field he chose. The borrower would start thinking of Marius as a kindly uncle. Then the light bulb would go on over his head. Finally he would ask if Marius could loan him money. You know what Marius' answer always was.

After 1955 Miller managed to see that Marius never got a whole lot of money in his hands, so his losses were limited. He even managed to loan to a few nice people who wanted to repay the loans. In 1962 Marius got into some trouble, and Miller took a bunch of these loans into the trust. At that time Miller got a little worried about his father possibly revoking the revocable trust. Although it had some unfavorable tax consequences, Miller created an irrevocable trust and placed all of the investment grade assets therein. He left all of Marius' investments in the old trust. Miller had also separated Helena's community interest in the original trust in 1958. All assets were then separate property, and Miller had total control over all of the investment grade assets.

In addition to loaning money, Marius would buy all kinds of junk. He would plan to sell at a profit, but somehow the sale never happened.

I won a case with the IRS on this issue. They disallowed the losses from Marius' "business", claiming it was a hobby. I countered that the Internal Revenue Code specifies that the investor must have an intent to make a profit in order to claim a deduction. I argued that there is no place in the law that says that the intent can't be stupid. I concluded my argument by introducing the revenue agent to Marius. He caught on quickly.

One time Miller decided that he was going to round up a lot of this stuff and sell it at auction. He made all the arrangements to bring the stuff to a central point, and the auctioneer went to work. It was a bright idea, worthy of Miller. There was only one thing that could happen to thwart Miller, and it did. Marius started bidding on several of the lots and bought quite a few. Explaining it afterwards Marius said, "I had to buy them. The price was so cheap."

In 1967 I was already named as successor trustee after Miller. Then Miller talked to me about his will. By that time, Miller was quite wealthy. It is of great interest that W.J. and his son and grandson each went independently into the San Joaquin Valley and made over a million dollars in the farming business. True, W.J. set his sights too high and tried to do too much. The best you can say about Marius is that he was just plain lucky with Cheek and Hotchkiss. However, Miller made two fortunes for his father and himself and knew how to keep them. You have already seen the greatness of W.J. and the greatness of Miller. Marius' ineptitude is equally obvious. This is the story of a pair of kings and a joker.

Miller did not allow any wishful thinking when he discussed his will.

It was clear that I was his third choice in terms of ability, and he was blunt about it, "I have a new will, and I have to choose an executor.

If I had a free choice, I would choose George Wightman, but I am not sure that I can trust George. The other person that I would choose before you is your brother Bill, but I am not sure that he would get around to doing anything. So that leaves you."

I had no idea at the time that I would soon become executor, but Miller did. I became executor early in 1968 after Miller's suicide.

CHAPTER 31

EPIPHANY

Sometimes I wonder if Miller really had a clever plan to give me added motivation. Anyway the result would not have been any different. Miller left me a large volume of written instructions. I worked so hard to do what he had wanted, following his plan. Everybody was helpful. Phil Farrar even introduced me to his real estate broker, Ed Weeks. Ed had executed all of the sales of the Firebaugh Farms land that Phil had bought. He eventually sold Miller's ranch for me. Floyd Phillips, the ranch foreman, and all of the other employees were wonderful. It all helped me to follow Miller's plan.

After a couple of months had passed, I was sitting in the office with Floyd on one side and Ed on the other. Ed wanted to remove the barley crop because it looked ratty and was hurting his efforts to sell the ranch. Floyd wanted to let the crop mature more, develop a lower moisture content, and therefore sell at a higher price. Each one looked at me, waiting for the decision. I dutifully asked myself, "What would Miller do?"

My thought process then ran sort of like this, "There is nothing in Miller's instructions that covers this situation. I don't know what Miller would do...and Miller doesn't know either, because he stopped thinking about the ranch two months ago. He does not know anything about what has been happening the last two months. I am the only one in this situation who has the decision making authority. I am in charge. Miller is not. Still, I want very much to do this job well. It is my responsibility. I want to get more information before I make this decision. I have a feeling that I will have to make many more decisions like this."

My trance only lasted a few seconds. When I came out of it, I started a discussion with Floyd about how barley is priced. That led into discussion of how much new money we could pick up by lowering moisture content over various periods of time. The window actually showed. I don't remember the exact numbers, but I do recall that there was a lot to gain by waiting two weeks and much less additional gain by waiting one week after that. I wanted to keep the period low to keep Ed happy but still give Floyd recognition. I proceeded to sweet talk Ed into accepting the two week delay, and the job was done.

Over the following eighteen months I made several decisions. Sometimes I made everybody happy. Sometimes I made nobody happy. Sometimes I screwed up, I am sure. Nevertheless, the ranch got managed and eventually sold. The probate of Miller's estate was eventually concluded.

The change in me was subtle, not overpowering. I still carry most of my weaknesses. There are still many things that I simply can not do well. However, it is now almost forty years that I have not hidden from responsibility, and I have not been afraid to make difficult decisions. My life has been better for it.

I have told the "barley story" many times since it happened. Every time I tell it I am thrilled all over again. This could have been what Miller was pointing me toward. I did the job; I was trustworthy; and I kept at it until it was done. When I first told the story, I used to say, "Miller Hotchkiss died so that I could be saved." This was too heavy a comment for most people to take. I abandoned the line but I have never abandoned the thought. Thank you, Miller. I know I will be able to thank you in person someday.

I went on to perform my newly established skills as executor in several other estates:

Helena Hotchkiss	1968
Ethel Hotchkiss	1969
Bill Hotchkiss	1972
Marius Hotchkiss	1974

In 1972 I established a business in which I managed trusts and investment assets in addition to accounting and tax planning for non-family clients. Just to prove that you don't lose the touch, I did the estate of Dorothy Wightman Hood in 2005. Dear Cousin Dotty, now I am the only one remaining of the ten grandchildren.

CHAPTER 32

ETHEL HOTCHKISS ESTATE

Linville Lee Hotchkiss was the youngest of the five children of W.J. Hotchkiss. He was the third to die, after Homer in 1924 and J.M. in 1952. Linville's only son, Pete died in World War II in 1944. After his divorce from Margaret, Linville married Ethel Trout. Ethel inherited everything from Linville when he died November 21, 1962.

Ethel died in 1969. She was a nice lady. When she didn't tell the truth, which was quite often, it was quite harmless. Miller Hotchkiss really liked Ethel. He thought that she was fun to be around, so he maintained a friendship with her. When Ethel and Linville traveled to Tasmania, the newspaper reported that America's largest stamp collector from the United States had come to their shores. They were happy to create a major article, but of course none of it was true. Anyway Ethel was always interesting.

I was busy probating Miller's estate and Helena's estate. I was also setting up trusts and running the East Side Ranch, when all of a sudden along came Ethel. Ethel had inherited from Linville. There was a rather obscure section of the probate code in California that said that if the wife dies subsequently, and the estate consists of what had been separate property of the husband, that property comes back to the husband's family. Well wasn't that interesting for the Hotchkiss family!

Section 229 of the California Probate Code was a revelation to me. Since I was already very busy being an executor and trustee, it was natural that I would serve as co-executor of Ethel's estate. Obviously we had to have someone from the Trout family as well. I never met any of the others, but Dick Trout was the co-executor. After some discussion Dick and I properly assumed that we would get a square deal from Mel Morgan, who was the attorney representing the estate. At that time Janin, Morgan and Brenner had a fellow named Mike Curtis, who was a very brilliant attorney, working for them. He was assigned to this probate. I knew that it would be better if I didn't get involved with the decision making for this estate. I wanted to leave it as a situation where two nice guys, Dick Trout and I, had decided to entrust our fate to the hands of Janin, Morgan and Brenner, which in this case was Mike Curtis. Even though I was very close to Mel Morgan, I also saw quite a bit of Mike

Curtis and other members of that firm, in my various other capacities of executor and trustee. Whenever the opportunity arose, I would say "Ethel Hotchkiss' estate, Mike Curtis is the executor". I encouraged Mike to take the lead but he didn't need very much encouragement. He sized up the situation the same way I did.

I did get to see the bed that Rudolf Valentino slept in. Of course that was just another one of Ethel's fun stories. As if I needed verification, Dick Trout explained that she very seldom told the truth. There were approximately 21 silver containers, which held salt, pepper, and oil and vinegar for dressing a salad. They were all lined up on one side of the kitchen and I thought, "Oh boy, this stuff is valuable. I am not going to touch any of it." Dick arranged for a lot of it to be taken away and sold. I don't know how it came out in real value or what actually was recorded in the estate. Even if my family never got a cent from any valuation of the household goods, I felt I was doing real fine, and representing my family also.

Some bonds were missing, we never did find them. I was sort of proud about the stocks. I determined exactly what stock certificates should be in the safety deposit box, the name of the company and the number of shares. I did it just by using my dividend reporting service and copies of Ethel's tax returns. Ethel had two separate safe deposit boxes, one for bonds and one for stocks. I guess she thought that she should never commingle stocks and bonds. The stock box was opened and every share of stock was there and accounted for. There is not much else to report. Everything went relatively harmoniously.

The law was perfectly clear about what should go to the Hotchkiss family. That does not mean that juries always pay attention to the law. Mel Morgan described it as one of those cases that if it went to the jury, it would take the jury about ten seconds to decide against the Hotchkiss family, even though the law was very clear. Ethel had brought nothing to the marriage of any consequence. For strategic reasons, during the probate of Linville's estate, some of the property had been declared to be Ethel's property or community property. What did this mean? It meant that representing the family in my fiduciary capacity, I could lay my hands on a lot of assets for my extended family, possibly all of Ethel's estate. It meant that if I got greedy and tried to lay my hands on too many assets, I could lose the whole ball of wax if it went to a jury. I was not sure what to do.

Mel Morgan, who often times thinks like a judge rather than an attorney, pontificated quite a bit. He eventually said, "It seems to me that there would have been seven surviving siblings in Ethel and Linville's family. Let's assume that they all came from the same family. Three of these children were Trout's and four of the children were Hotchkisses. So four sevenths would go to the Hotchkiss family and three sevenths would go to the Trout family."

Actually, there were three Trout heirs and four sets of Hotchkiss heirs. It was something for me to hang my hat on, so I took it back to the family. I said basically, "It's found money. There could easily be nothing. You guys better support me and accept this." They did.

I think Dick Trout probably felt the same way. His family agreed also. I'm still not sure how I did what I did with Marius. It was basically standard estate planning practice for somebody who had an estate over one million dollars and who was well over eighty to decline to accept the inheritance and pass it on to his heirs. The technical word is disclaim. I managed to convince Marius that this was the right thing to do. He really didn't need the money, and he should just let the rest of the family have it. I explained to him that I had a share of it, but I'm sure he knew that I was a deserving person. Nobody ever told him that the division was one third to Emmy Lou, one sixth to me, one sixth to my brother's family. The remaining third went to Hazel Wightman, who immediately disclaimed her inheritance in favor of her five children. In addition to what she inherited from Uncle Marius, Emmy Lou also received her one seventh share directly from Ethel's estate.

I never really understood why George Wightman got involved in Ethel's estate. He threatened at the beginning to take part in the management. I didn't want him looking over my shoulder. Besides, I knew he was going to try to grind his ax over having each of W.J.'s ten grandchildren inherit equally. George formally requested special notice. This meant that he would receive a copy of every document that was filed with the court.

Actually, George and his four siblings did quite well. Since Ethel died intestate, her estate on the Hotchkiss side was distributed one fourth to each of the remaining Hotchkiss families. Hazel got her one fourth. Then she turned around and received another third of Marius' disclaimer. This was all done under the laws of the State of California concerning intestacy.

George Wightman, in fairness to him, had seen this problem in his other families. They were all sort of prolific and by the time anything got divided up, there were minute shares coming down to each individual in the families that had been most prolific.

George had been President of Northwestern Leather Company, a pretty good-sized family operation. He had been one of the three family members who organized and structured the liquidation of the Hotchkiss Estate Company. He was intelligent. He had been a vice president of a fairly large public corporation. His weakness was a refusal to let go when it was appropriate. In some cases this trait was to be admired. He had a major stroke and when he came back from it he came back with Noel Coward records. He played the records for hours on end, because he didn't want to lose his proper Bostonian accent.

CHAPTER 33

HOW COULD HE BE THE SON OF W.J.?

It is sometimes hard to believe that W.J. and Marius were father and son. They were such totally different people. It was not just the difference between W.J.'s success and Marius' lack of same. Everything about them was different.

W.J. of course lived with borrowed money. He never drove. There was something said that he had an accident early in his life and he never drove since, but he never lacked for drivers. Herb Cheek was driving him down to the Central Valley from the bay area. They passed through this little town along the way and all of a sudden W.J. says, "Stop the car; stop the car; stop the car!" Bewildered, Herb stopped. W.J. said "I'll be right back," and he walked into a small bank. After a few minutes he walked back again and Herb said, "W.J. what was that all about?" W.J. said, "I saw that bank. It's one of the banks that I've never borrowed any money from." Herb said, "Did you get any from them?" W.J. said, "Oh yes, drive on."

Marius never borrowed money, because he wasn't sure how to do it. In the days when he was farming for his own account the bank prepared all of the papers for routine crop loans. After 1954 Marius always had money, but it burned a hole in his pocket. He became more of a lender than a borrower.

W.J. worked with the real power players in the Central Valley. Once, he and Sam Irvine (This is Sam Irvine of the Irvine ranch and a few hundred million dollars, whereas all W.J. got was effective bankruptcy) were bidding on a tract of land in a public sale. W.J. kept bidding up the price, and finally, Sam Irvine just quit. W.J. bought the property. As they were walking out of the room, Sam Irvine turned to W.J. and said, "W.J., the water for that land goes through my property, I'm turning it off tomorrow morning."

It seemed as if Marius deliberately sought out the very minor players in the game. The business relationship usually started out with a loan from Marius. From there it sometimes grew into a disastrous business venture.

W.J. had a great sense of humor. When he was in the political arena, he could strip away all the trappings, revealing the heart of the issue, and then make a joke out of it. When he worked on the planning for the Golden Gate Bridge, he was responsible for a wonderful quote. "When we agreed to work together for the bridge, everybody vowed to keep politics completely out of the picture. This guide has been followed, except of course in San Francisco."

Even in his later years, W.J. was ready with a quip. His home telephone had a number similar to that of a nearby movie theatre. Callers sometimes responded to W.J.'s "hello", with a question, "Oaks Theatre?" W.J. happily replied, "Nothing playing tonight," and hung up.

Marius inherited the lack of humor from his mother. In reality, he was much too busy creating lies to support his position. He never had the time to create humor consciously. Of course, he created a lot of humor inadvertently, but people were quietly laughing at him rather than with him. Marius was so unswerving in his peculiar behavior that those who knew him just went with the flow.

W.J was a man of strength, who pursued great dreams. Marius was a man of neurosis who dreamed up lies and never succeeded well at anything. A rough diamond, he played baseball and played it pretty well, but never professionally. In the course of things he got into some funny neurotic patterns. He never opened his Christmas packages. Everyone else would open theirs and say thank you, while Marius would just take the package in hand and put it down by his chair. He never opened his Christmas presents because he didn't know how to say thank you. He never ever left a tip in a restaurant, because he wasn't sure how much to leave.

The grandchildren always called it "The Big House". This was where W.J and Emma lived. The expansive layout was described in an earlier chapter. It had half a dozen bedrooms, a full attic and a cupola on top of the whole mess. There were three "living rooms". The family lived in one. The second was a game room. Nobody knew what the third one was for, because it was never used. The other half of the ground floor was dedicated to a dining room, a gigantic pass-pantry, and the world's largest kitchen. Everybody ate at a large table in the kitchen. I am not sure how often the dining room was used. I do know that when the family was growing up, Emma always had two giant wheels of cheese on the dining room table so that her children could have a snack when they came home.

Probably at Emma's instigation, W.J. deeded building lots at the opposite end of their property, on Domingo Avenue. J.M. and Linville had corner lots on Domingo and what became Hazel Road. There was a road of sorts going through before Hazel Road was improved and officially dedicated in 1940. Marius had the next house down, toward the "Big House", from Linville. Each of them built their own homes on the property. It was interesting that Linville's wife always wanted a patio, so there was a lovely large patio inside the outer walls.

Marius got some men from the ranch to build his house. He brought crews from Firebaugh and put them to work. Of course they never heard of compacting fill, so on this slight downgrade, the house settled. You could put a marble on the floor in the living room, and it would roll all the way to the downhill corner. Outside of this little problem, the house looked pretty good. Helena wanted Colonial style, and that is what she got.

Under Marius' tender care the house aged poorly. He built a sewing room for Helena off of the master bedroom on the second floor. It looked horrid, was not quite level, and Helena was afraid to walk into it for fear that it would fall to the ground.

White with green shutters looked beautiful in 1931, but the original paint job didn't look so good in 1965. The neighbors started pleading for a new paint job. Miller pleaded with Marius to call in a painter. Marius said there was nothing wrong with the paint. The standoff continued into my period of management. Suddenly one day Marius told me that he had decided to repaint the house. I waited for the next sentence, hoping he was not planning to use purple. Not to worry, Marius said he thought the original color was best. Of course, it didn't really make any difference. He started stalling and eventually abandoned the project.

Back in 1965 the neighbor across the street complained to Miller that Marius came out of the house to pick up his morning paper without wearing any pants. They said this was a terrible thing for their teen age daughter to see out of her bedroom window. Miller responded not very gently that the daughter should pull her shade down instead of up. This bounced back on me a few years later. I was very concerned about Marius, who continued to insist on living alone. I called the neighbors to ask them just to keep an eye out for Marius and report any news to me. The neighbor with the daughter said she was much too busy to do that, and by the way, I should get the house painted.

After W.J died in 1936 Marius got a truck and some ranch workers and came close to stripping W.J.'s house. He took lots of the fine antique furniture and put it all in his house. In a family there are some things that once they are done they are done. Marius knew that. He was intelligent, just very aggressive, very neurotic and very peculiar. He could execute a double squeeze in bridge but on the next hand he would play the wrong card out of his hand and think nothing of it.

In 1967, Helena had a series of strokes. As her life became simplified, every time she saw me it reminded her of the same story that she always told. It was a pretty good story, however I don't know if it's true or not. Miller Hotchkiss was sixteen years older than me. I was a bright lad and I was walking back up the hill from grandfather's house, walking past Marius and Helena's house. Miller was standing out in front watering the lawn. He lifted the hose, pointed it towards the road and started to sprinkle me. According to Helena's story, I turned to Miller and said, "Miller, don't be a damn fool."

As Helena's condition worsened, it got to the point that Helena couldn't fight back at Marius any more, and Marius missed this. Part of his life was being yelled at. Miller stepped in at this point and asked Cousin Eva Lee to come and make a home for Helena and Marius.

Eva Lee Calhoun was the daughter of Luther Grove.[see *The Millionaire Miner and the Indian Girl* by James M. Hotchkiss, Jr.] Luther Grove was the one who cared for John Hite in his last days, living in the apartment where John lived. John Hite, the millionaire miner, was Emma's uncle. Eva Lee was there when the second codicil of John's will was signed. She said once, "Oh I could tell you stories about how they had to keep him alive for 48 hours so that it seemed that he hadn't signed that codicil on his death bed." Eva Lee had her share of experiences. I refer to her from time to time in the John Hite book. She had married Harry Calhoun and lived next door to the Hotchkiss ranch. Harry Calhoun died young, as they say, leaving a wife and three children. Eva Lee, the widow, ran the prune ranch. After a while she sold the ranch and moved to the city. At the time of Helena's illness, Eva Lee had no particular source of income. On the other hand, she wasn't impoverished either. She was very fond of Helena.

Eva Lee was not a fool. Her first action was to sound the death knell for the terrible mattresses. Once Isabel and I had to sleep on them and I'll tell you, we just didn't get much sleep that night. Eva Lee wandered through the house, on an inspection tour, and said that she would take the job, offered to her by Miller. There was one demand that she had. The mattresses had to be replaced with new mattresses and springs, which they were. This was the end of the mattress saga and the beginning of the Eva Lee saga.

It was really too bad that Eva Lee had never liked Marius. She considered Helena her good friend. She told her daughter that the only reason she took the job was to help protect Helena from Marius.

With Marius she gave as good as she got. Marius must have felt he was in heaven, but it was terribly hard on Eva Lee. Eventually, Helena had to be hospitalized, where she died early in 1968, a short month after her son.

Eva Lee seized Helena's institutionalization as her opportunity to leave. She had totally zero interest in making a home for Marius. If Helena was not around, Eva Lee was not going to be there either. After she left, she passed on one of my favorite anecdotes.

Marius stole from himself. There was an antique shop in the commercial district, about a block and a half away. Marius would take some of the beautiful antiques that they had in the house. It seemed like dishes and silverware primarily, stuff that you could carry easily. He would take it to the antique dealer and sell it for cash. Later Eva Lee would go up to the dealer and buy it back. The whole thing made no sense, but there was a lot about Marius that made no sense. Eva Lee existed there and she and Marius yelled at each other. Since she never liked Marius anyway, she left after Helena was institutionalized.

Marius learned one thing from his mother; you never tell the truth if a lie will serve you better. Marius had a mistress, who apparently was a very nice lady according to Marius' friends. She was from the Knightsen area but living in Oakland. Marius had known her from the Knightsen days, over forty years earlier. Every time she and Marius got together they always started yelling and screaming at each other. I guess that was true till the end. There was some problem because Marius had bought her a car. I didn't see any record that he had done anything else, but he did buy the car. This was before Miller died, and he was looking into it. She had been the mistress for quite a while. One day she shot and killed herself. Miller didn't know if there was going to be a big scandal, but nothing ever came of it.

Marius was in the junk business. In those days, Miller always referred to Marius and his "junky friends." This was long before "junky" acquired its current meaning. Marius put 20,000 miles on his car every year, but he never left the Bay Area. I know this is true, because I read the mileage indicator. He would go from junkyard to junkyard where he knew these various people. That world was one in which cash was essentially lacking. The junk dealers would trade with each other, but never bought anything for cash.

Well, along came Marius. I don't mean to say that they cheated him, but he had cash. When W.J. was dying and called for Miller at his bedside, he told Miller what should be done with each of his children. He said, "Marius should never have cash." Marius had cash, so he bought things, I kept track of his financial investments and they were dogs. Marius had no concept of what a product was or how to do business. He would buy a ton of aluminum rods. You had to cut them up to make them saleable. So let's say Marius bought the aluminum for the equivalent of five cents per finished rod. And he paid five cents for each rod to be cut up. When they were all cut up and finished, he sold them for six cents and then boasted that he had made a profit on the deal. That was Marius in business. Miller was of course, rightfully furious.

I met Mrs. Ed Covell at a bridge tournament. She didn't know who I was. After being introduced she said, "Oh I know a man named Hotchkiss." Then as she leaned back she said, "He's loaded."

This was a good description. Ed Covell was a pretty good guy, but in that business problems do come up. Marius hadn't seen Ed in quite some time and Marius was playing gin rummy in the junkyard office with Hank Martin.(That's Mrs. Martin. Virgil was her husband.) Ed Covell drove into the yard and said, "Marius, what do you want for that pile of aluminum?"

Marius said, "Not for sale."

Ed Covell said, "I really need aluminum right now, I can pay you top dollar for it."

However, Marius still responded, "Not for sale."

Finally, Ed named a price and named a price so high that Marius grudgingly agreed. Ed loaded his truck with the aluminum. As he stopped at the office, he leaned his head out the truck window and said, "Marius, I'm going to take this aluminum and not pay you for it, and that makes up for the time that you used my T.D. tractor and didn't pay me." Ed waltzed out of the driveway with the aluminum.

Marius turned to Hank and said, "But he can't do that can he?"

Hank said, "He just did."

When I wrote the first draft of this chapter I gave it to my assistant to file. She was not a good speller, but maybe she knew something. She named the file, "family anticdotes".

CHAPTER 34

THE KINGS ARE GONE, BUT THE JOKER IS STILL WILD

I was trustee for Marius for six years from 1968 until his death in 1974. It was really quite easy for me. Miller had already done all of the tough work. For some reason, Marius never yelled at me. Maybe it was because I never interfered in his affairs unless I absolutely had to. It was unlikely that I would have to. The days when he had a lot of cash in his pocket were gone. I saw that he always had some cash. Of course, it got dribbled away, but it was nothing in the grand scheme of things.

Barbara and Roger Phipps had been installed in the home to care for Marius after Eva Lee Calhoun left. This was so typically Miller. He bought a home in Sacramento for Roger and Barbara in exchange for their agreeing to make a home for Marius as long as he lived. Roger was just out of the military, retired as a sergeant. He was married to Barbara, who was a delightful person. My brother Bill's house, which he had inherited from our father, was kitty-corner across the street. Bill's wife, Peggy, got along really well with Barbara. Both of them kept me alert to what Marius was doing or not doing.

Barbara Phipps was Helena's niece, the oldest daughter of Helena's sister, Lillian. She was Miller's first cousin. Roger ended up as Marius' driver with Barbara as the homemaker. I saw Barbara many times and she had these wonderful anecdotes about Marius. My favorite one was about the incinerator.

When they put up Linville's house they planted a hedge, but they planted it right on the property line. The hedge grew up of course, and went about two feet into Marius' property. This was okay except Marius' incinerator had been built a foot or two from the property line and was now engulfed by the hedge. No one was stupid enough to light the incinerator. That didn't mean that it hadn't been filled with paper and odd trash. Whenever Marius went out he wanted to have a piece of paper with him in order to write things down such as deals that he was going to make. Barbara said, "You know, Jim, he uses the incinerator as a filing cabinet. Whenever he goes out, he stops there and picks a piece of paper out of the incinerator, puts it in his pocket and takes it with him."

Marius never took a bath. I don't know if that came from his mother forcing him to take a bath on Saturday night, whether he needed it or not. Once, during a very seldom Berkeley heat wave, Marius got into the shower, turned the water on but never used any soap, he came out, got dressed and told Barbara, It was the way to keep cool, go in the shower.

Of course, Roger never yelled at Marius and Marius never yelled at Roger. It was all between Marius and Barbara. Barbara did not have the ability to yell back, and she took a lot after Helena died. Marius began to sell or give away Helena's things. He happily told Barbara that Helena's mink coat would go to Polly McMaster, because she knew how to wear things like that and Barbara didn't. Polly had gone to the Opera once, so Polly could wear the mink to the Opera. Barbara took it in stride, but the tension started to develop. Eventually it exploded.

Barbara took it all, letting out steam whenever she got a chance to talk to Peggy. Roger was the designated driver for Marius, from junkyard to junkyard all day. Marius never ate lunch, which meant that Roger never had a chance to eat lunch. He had no ulcers when he started working for Marius. The ulcers were earned on the job.

Whenever Marius stopped anywhere, his car stopped too. It didn't bother Marius if Roger went to the bathroom, because Marius just got in the car and drove himself. Not having a driver's license any more was not a concern to him. One fatal day, Roger talked back to Marius, for the first time. He said his ulcers were killing him, and he had to take time to eat something. Marius fired him on the spot. He then drove home and fired Barbara also. There was no chance to reverse the judgment.

Marius had a pet phrase he used, "and that's the answer!" The next day Marius came into my office and told me that he got rid of Roger. As Marius explained it to me, "Roger told me he wanted to have lunch now, and I told him that I had to go some place. He told me he wanted to stop and have lunch. He talked back to me, and that's the answer, right now!" It was irreversible. Barbara and Roger left in August, 1968. Until his death in 1974 Marius lived alone.

Leroy drove for Marius for a while when I was in charge. However, that didn't work out. Marius fired Leroy. Leroy would take the car home at night. I said, "Marius why did you fire Leroy?"

Marius just looked at me. You could never tell if what he was saying was the truth or not. He said, "The car ended up parked in front of too many pool halls."

Marius still had Alma, the maid. Apparently, she got along quite well with Marius. She sponge bathed him when he was going out. He sat down in a chair, and she would bathe him down to his waist. I saw that a couple of times. It was not a time for me to rock the boat by trying to replace Alma. Marius would have driven off anybody that I employed, anyway. Peggy Hotchkiss remained my source of information.

Alma was the long time housekeeper for Helena and subsequently for Marius. Miller hated Alma. He said that she never cleaned, and the house was always filthy dirty. He didn't know that Alma also stole. Marius had promised her a car before he died. I bought it for her because his promise had been clear. Frankly I was afraid, as were other members of the family, that Alma would burn down the house or something. She stole the couch, and when we pointed out to her that the couch wasn't there, she looked directly at Peggy and me and said, "There never was a couch there." Helena's fine crystal punch bowl never existed either.

Did Marius believe in God? Probably not. He never mentioned religion to me. Surely, he must have had one glorious moment that he believed that God would part the waters for him. One day there was a lot of rain. Hazel Road is one block long and shaped somewhat like the letter "V". The highest ground is at each end, and the lowest point is where the creek runs under the road. That day the creek decided to run also on top of the road. In fact, the police were present with warning lights and barricades. The water depth at the bottom of the road was a couple of feet.

Around the barricade obliviously came Marius. The creek was in the way of his getting home. Surely it would stop or part for him. The creek did neither, and Marius stopped ignominiously. The incident was a true test for young Bill Hotchkiss who had just brought his future wife home to meet his parents. Carole is a very bright lady. Her very first words in the situation were, "Bill, who is that crazy fool down there?"

Bill showed courage but not pride as he grudgingly admitted, "That's my Uncle Marius."

By that time Peggy had also noticed what had happened. She walked toward the car, which was unmoving. Marius got out of the car and took a few steps up the hill to get out of the water. He then handed the car keys to Peggy, saying, "Here honey, you take care of it." He then trudged up the street to his house.

Just think how nice Marius was to everybody who has heard this story. If he had driven around the block and entered Hazel Road from the other side, he would have gotten home routinely, and we would not have had a chance to enjoy this incredible tale.

George Wightman appeared on the scene again in 1974. Burning a hole inside of him was the fact that if Marius died intestate, one third of everything he owned would go to Emmy Lou. One third was going to be divided among George and his four other siblings. It didn't strike George as being rather equitable.

Actually, Marius had a will. Miller had forced him to make one earlier. The only thing wrong was that the only people named were Miller and Helena, both of whom were dead. Effectively, Marius had no will. Dutifully, I reminded Marius of this every year, but he totally ignored me. Many people are like this where their last wishes are discussed.

George had a habit of doing these things in his mother's name. He would start out with, "Mother suggested it to me," or "I talked to Mother and she said." So George wrote Marius a letter, it said that Mother wanted you to know that if you die without a will, one half would go to Jim and Emmy Lou. Only one third would be divided among Mother, her five children and her umpteen grandchildren and umpteen great grandchildren. He named the numbers, and they were considerable.

Marius came storming into my office and threw the letter on my desk. He said, "What's that all about?"

I looked at it and said "Well Marius, it's true and that's the way it is. If you want it to be different you have to make a will." He mumbled something unintelligible and stormed out. There I was, holding this burning paper in my hand. The first thing I did was go to the copy machine, make a copy of it and mail it to Emmy Lou. Emmy Lou from that time forward always referred to George as her former cousin. It was a typical Emmy Lou line.

That could have been the end of it, but George was persistent. He came to California to handle this matter directly. I didn't know him before the stroke, but after the stroke he was very frank about what he intended to do. He told me, "I am going to Marius, and I am going to talk to him about the unfairness about what would happen with his money going to Emmy Lou.

I said, "George, these are the laws of the State of California. That's the way it works without a will".

"No!" he said, "that's not fair for Mother". He began naming grandchildren and great grandchildren. I asked what he was going to do and he said, "I am going to go to Marius. I am going to talk to him and I am going to stay there all day and talk to him. If he hasn't decided to make a will, I will come back the next day and talk to him".

I don't know how much of a dent he made. I have since seen the same result in my professional practice. This was the first time that I saw it, and I didn't recognize what was going to happen. Marius was dead within a week. I have seen other older people killed by their heirs, just from the pressure that was placed on them. I'm sure that George was honest in his intentions and had a cause, but I also feel that Marius, who was only 89 years old when he died, may have lived longer if George had not pressured him.

Marius died in the late afternoon, sitting in his chair, waiting for his bridge partner to pick him up. He died apparently in his sleep. The police were called. Of course the fire department had been called also, and the other official type people were all bustling around. I took the opportunity to go to the telephone. I called Emmy Lou and I said, "Emmy Lou, I have some sad news for you, Uncle Marius just died". In sympathy, Emmy Lou said, "Poor old mean, terrible, nasty Uncle Marius".

I called George and told him that Uncle Marius had died. I left it to him when his mother should be told. He said that he would take care of it and also notify Mother's several other children and grandchildren and great grandchildren.

Marius' death, before he could make a new will, de-fanged George. He had no other power source to work from. He showed hostility by asking for special notice in Marius' estate, just as in Ethel Hotchkiss' estate. He never really took any action and disappeared from the power scene. I guess I did my homework well.

George had taken up with Kitty, a very nice young lady, several years his junior. Cousin Dotty described the relationship as, "Kitty is a nice girl who needs a father". George announced that he was making a visit to the west coast with Kitty. No one else in the family wanted to bother to welcome him. I was the only one. George certainly was not my favorite, but he was my cousin and was entitled to my attention. We didn't talk about the family history or Marius' death. We talked about paintings, how to play tennis, and his mother and what a great tennis player she was. I haven't mentioned earlier, but George played elegant cocktail piano. He was extremely good at it, and Emmy Lou just loved to listen to him play.

On March 19, 1974 I wrote to Emmy Lou:

All is sweetness and light with a certain eastern relative to whom I just spoke on the phone. He says he understands that certain actions that Marius might have taken are now a closed issue. He also told me that he had been in conference with "Motah" – Motah told him that,
"Jim should handle Marius' estate and that Emmy Lou should help him."

George then added (from George),"This would help justify Emmy Lou's getting one third."

In May Emmy Lou wrote to me:

"I trust you have recovered from George's visitation [with Kitty] which I dreaded for you. I think by now you've built a valuable insulation so you can tune him out entirely. In part I think the sins he sees in western cousins have something to do with our capacity for having a good time. Pleasure is suspect! Oh well, it's too late to stop enjoying ourselves and assume the mantles of martyrdom."

Emmy Lou also wrote to me shortly after George's death on February 16, 1978:

"The mind is conveniently shaped to remember what it wants to, so I shall probably be thinking kind thoughts about George. From not thinking of him at all for a long time, his death has caused me to move backward into memories of Peter, Miller, Bill and the whole of life's fragility. I wish I could offer words of comfort and wisdom to our Wightman cousins in place of the dull little notes I have just written to them.

"There are always so many things that never quite get said – out of shyness or fear of sounding sentimental. Therefore I take this opportunity while alive, well and in reasonable mental health, to tell you I love you dearly and could not devise a kinder funnier cousin."

Today in 2008 it is too late to say "thank you" to Emmy Lou and to all of the other family members for their contributions to my life. Instead I say in the privacy of my room, "Thank you all, every one of you including Marius and George. My life has been richer because of you. Maybe that's what it's all about."

A final word about Marius. He died in peace, knowing that he had never done anything wrong in his life. And that's the answer, right now!